Shakespeare in Love

SHAKESPEARE IN LOVE

A SCREENPLAY

MARC NORMAN AND TOM STOPPARD

HYPERION
MIRAMAX BOOKS
NEW YORK

Photographs by Laurie Sparham

 Printed in the United States of America. For information address: Hyperion, 114 Fifth Ave, New York, New York 10011.

ISBN 0-7394-0317-6

Shakespeare in Love

INT. THE ROSE THEATRE. DAY.

*SKY. Over which a title "*LONDON—SUMMER 1593*" appears.*

Title card: In the glory days of the Elizabethan theatre two playhouses were fighting it out for writers and audiences. North of the city was the Curtain Theatre, home to England's most famous actor, Richard Burbage. Across the river was the competition, built by Philip Henslowe, a businessman with a cash flow problem . . .

. . . The Rose . . .

Gradually a building is revealed, The Rose Theatre; three-tiered, open to the elements and empty. On the floor, roughly printed, a poster—torn, soiled, out of date. It says:

SEPT. 7TH & 8TH AT NOON
MR. EDWARD ALLEYN AND THE ADMIRAL'S MEN AT THE ROSE THEATRE, BANKSIDE
THE LAMENTABLE TRAGEDIE OF THE MONEYLENDER REVENG'D

OVER THIS the screams of a man under torture.

The screams are coming from the curtained stage.

VOICE (O.S.)
You Mongrel! Why do you howl
When it is I who am bitten?

INT. THE ROSE THEATRE. STAGE. DAY.

The theatre owner, PHILIP HENSLOWE, is the man screaming. HENSLOWE'S boots are on fire. He is pinioned in a chair, with his feet stuck out over the hot coals of a fire burning in a brazier. He is being held in that position by LAMBERT, who is a thug employed by FENNYMAN, who is the owner of the VOICE. The fourth man, FREES, is FENNYMAN'S bookkeeper.

FENNYMAN
What am I, Mr. Lambert?

LAMBERT

Bitten, Mr. Fennyman.

FENNYMAN

How badly bitten, Mr. Frees?

FREES

Twelve pounds, one shilling and four pence, Mr. Fennyman, including interest.

HENSLOWE

Aaagh! I can pay you!

FENNYMAN

When?

HENSLOWE

Two weeks, three at the most, Aaagh!
For pity's sake

FENNYMAN

Take his feet out. Where will you get . . .

FREES

(the mathematical genius with a notebook)

Sixteen pounds, five shillings and nine pence . . .

FENNYMAN

. . . including interest in three weeks?

HENSLOWE

I have a wonderful new play!

FENNYMAN

Put his feet in.

HENSLOWE

It's a comedy.

FENNYMAN

Cut his nose off.

HENSLOWE

A new comedy. By Will Shakespeare!

FENNYMAN

And his ears.

HENSLOWE

And a share. We will be partners, Mr. Fennyman!

FENNYMAN

(hesitating)

Partners?

HENSLOWE

It's a crowd-tickler—mistaken identities, a shipwreck, a pirate king, a bit with a dog, and love triumphant.

LAMBERT

I think I've seen it. I didn't like it.

HENSLOWE

This time it is by Shakespeare.

FENNYMAN

What's the title?

HENSLOWE

Romeo and Ethel the Pirate's Daughter.

FENNYMAN

Good title.

FENNYMAN snaps his fingers at FREES and LAMBERT. LAMBERT unties HENSLOWE, FREES starts writing a contract.

FENNYMAN (Cont'd)

A play takes time. Find actors . . . rehearsals . . . let's say open in three weeks. That's—what—five hundred groundlings at tuppence each, in addition four hundred backsides at three pence—a penny extra for a cushion, call it two hundred cushions, say two performance for safety—how much is that Mr. Frees?

FREES

Twenty pounds to the penny, Mr. Fennyman.

FENNYMAN

Correct!

HENSLOWE

But I have to pay the actors and the author.

FENNYMAN

A share of the profits.

HENSLOWE

There's never any . . .

FENNYMAN

Of course not!

HENSLOWE

(impressed)

Mr. Fennyman, I think you may have hit on something.

FENNYMAN slaps a contract down on the table next to an ink-pot and quill.

FENNYMAN

Sign here.

HENSLOWE takes the quill and signs.

FENNYMAN (Cont'd)

Romeo and Ethel The Pirate's Daughter . . . Almost finished?

HENSLOWE

Without doubt he is completing it at this very moment.

INT. WILL'S ROOM. DAY.

A small cramped space in the eaves of a building. A cluttered shelf containing various objects, wedged between crumpled pieces of paper. Among those we have time to observe: a skull, a mug that says A PRESENT FROM STRATFORD-UPON-AVON.

At infrequent intervals further pieces of crumpled paper are tossed towards the shelf. The man who is throwing them, WILL SHAKESPEARE, is bent over a table, writing studiously with a quill.

Now we see what he is writing: WILL is practising his signature, over and over again. "Will Shagsbeard . . . W Shakspur . . . William Shasper . . ." Each time he is dissatisfied, and each time he crumples, and tosses it away.

Suddenly WILL becomes impatient. He jumps up and goes to the loft area in the rafters, where he sleeps, and starts to pull on his boots. At this point the door opens and HENSLOWE walks in. He is out of breath and his feet hurt.

HENSLOWE

Will! Where is my play? Tell me you have it nearly done! Tell me you have it started.

(desperately)

You have begun?

WILL

(struggling with his boots)

Doubt that the stars are fire, doubt that the sun doth move . . .

HENSLOWE

No, no, we haven't the time. Talk prose. Where is my play?

WILL

(tapping his forehead and heading out the door)

It is all locked safe in here.

HENSLOWE

God be praised!

(then doubt)

Locked?

WILL

As soon as I have found my muse . . .

EXT. STREET. OUTSIDE WILL'S HOUSE. DAY.

WILL lives in a crowded area of the city. Hawkers are crying their wares, tract-sellers, delivery boys, and merchants go about their business. HENSLOWE catches up with WILL as he strides purposefully along.

HENSLOWE

(catching up)

Who is she this time?!

WILL

She is always Aphrodite.

HENSLOWE

Aphrodite Baggot who does it behind the Dog and Trumpet?

WILL

Henslowe, you have no soul so how can you understand the emptiness that seeks a soulmate?

HENSLOWE

Well, I am a dead man and buggered to boot. My theatre is closed by the plague these twelve weeks, my company is playing the inn-yards of England, while Burbage and the Chamberlain's Men are invited to court and receive ten pounds to play your piece, written for my theatre, by my writer, at my risk when you were green and grateful -

WILL

What piece? Richard Crookback?

HENSLOWE

No—it's comedy they want, Will! Comedy! Like *Romeo and Ethel*?

WILL

Who wrote that?

HENSLOWE

Nobody! You are writing it for me! I gave you three pounds a month since.

WILL

Half what you owed me. I am still due for *One Gentleman of Verona*.

EXT. ANOTHER STREET. DAY.

HENSLOWE'S hardly paused in his appeal.

HENSLOWE

. . . Will! What is money to you and me? I, your patron, you my wordwright! When the plague lifts Burbage will have a new Christopher Marlowe for the Curtain and I have nothing for the Rose.

WILL stops.

WILL

Mr. Henslowe, will you lend me fifty pounds?

HENSLOWE

(staggered)

Fifty pounds? What for?

WILL

Burbage offers me a partnership in the Chamberlain's Men. For fifty pounds my hired player days are over.

HENSLOWE

Cut out my heart! Throw my liver to the dogs!

WILL

(answering for him)

No, then.

WILL turns down a side street.

EXT. MARKETPLACE. DAY.

HENSLOWE and WILL are crossing a crowded marketplace where a Puritan preacher, MAKEPEACE, is haranguing anyone who will listen.

MAKEPEACE

. . . and the Lord shall smite them! Yea, harken to me. The theatres are handmaidens of the devil! Under the name of the Curtain, the players breed lewdness in your wives, rebellion in your servants, idleness in your apprentices and wickedness in your children! And the Rose smells thusly rank by any name! I say a plague on both their houses!

As he passes WILL gratefully makes a mental note.

EXT. DR. MOTH'S HOUSE. DAY.

WILL turns into a narrow street and walks toward a doorway.

HENSLOWE

Where are you going?

WILL

To my weekly confession.

As HENSLOWE arrives the door closes in his face. A sign identifies the place as the premises of DR. MOTH, apothecary, alchemist, astrologer, seer, interpreter of dreams, and priest of psyche. HENSLOWE looks puzzled.

INT. DR. MOTH'S HOUSE. DAY.

A stuffed alligator hangs from the ceiling; pills, potions, amulets and charms, star charts and mystic paraphernalia festoon the place. Testimonials and framed degrees hang on the walls.

WILL lying on a couch, on his back. His eyes are closed.

DR. MOTH sits by the couch, listening to WILL and occasionally making a note on a pad he holds on his knee. What we have here is nothing less than the false dawn of analysis. The session is being timed by an hourglass.

WILL

Words, words, words . . . once, I had the gift . . . I could make love out of words as a potter makes cups out of clay . . . love that overthrows empires, love that binds two hearts together come hellfire and brimstone . . . for sixpence a line, I could cause a riot in a nunnery . . . but now . . .

DR. MOTH

And yet you tell me you lie with women?

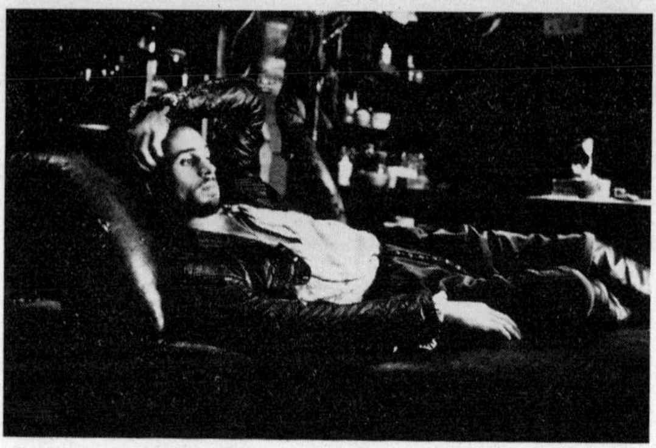

WILL seems unwilling to respond. DR. MOTH refers to his notes.

DR. MOTH (Cont'd)
Black Sue, Fat Phoebe, Rosaline, Burbage's seamstress; Aphrodite, who does it behind the Dog and . . .

WILL
(interrupting)
Aye, now and again, but what of it? I have lost my gift.

DR. MOTH
I am here to help you. Tell me in your own words.

WILL
I have lost my gift
(not finding this easy)
It's as if my quill is broken. As if the organ of the imagination has dried up. As if the proud tower of my genius has collapsed.

DR. MOTH
Interesting.

WILL
Nothing comes.

DR. MOTH
Most interesting.

WILL

(interrupting)

It is like trying to a pick a lock with a wet herring.

DR. MOTH

(shrewdly)

Tell me, are you lately humbled in the act of love?

WILL turns towards him. How did he know that?

DR. MOTH (Cont'd)

How long has it been?

WILL

A goodly length in times past, but lately—

DR. MOTH

No, no. You have a wife, children . . .

The sand runs through the hourglass.

LATER.

Not much sand left.

WILL

I was a lad of eighteen. Anne Hathaway was a woman, half as old again.

DR. MOTH

A woman of property?

WILL

(shrugs)

She had a cottage. One day, she was three months gone with child, so . . .

DR. MOTH

And your relations?

WILL

On my mother's side the Ardens . . .

DR. MOTH

No, your marriage bed.

WILL

Four years and a hundred miles away in Stratford. A cold bed too, since the twins were born. Banishment was a blessing.

DR. MOTH

So now you are free to love . . .

WILL

—yet cannot love nor write it.

DR. MOTH reaches for a glass snake bracelet.

DR. MOTH

Here is a bangle found in Psyche's temple on Olympus—cheap at four pence. Write your name on a paper and feed it in the snake.

WILL looks at the snake bangle in wonder.

WILL

Will it restore my gift?

DR. MOTH

The woman who wears the snake will dream of you, and your gift will return. Words will flow like a river. I will see you in a week.

He holds out his hand. WILL drops a sovereign into it, and takes the bracelet.

EXT. DR. MOTH'S HOUSE. DAY.

WILL comes out. HENSLOWE is waiting, standing in a horse trough to ease his feet. WILL walks straight past him, and HENSLOWE follows.

HENSLOWE

Now where? Will?

WILL

To the Palace at Whitehall.

INT. WHITEHALL PALACE. BACKSTAGE. DAY.

WHITEHALL means nothing yet. We are behind closed curtains on a stage busy with preparations for the imminent performance of Two Gentlemen of Verona. *This is not a theatre but a banqueting hall, as we will see.*

RICHARD BURBAGE is to play "PROTEUS." A BOY PLAYER will play "SILVIA," and last minute improvements to his makeup etc. are being applied by BURBAGE'S mistress ROSALINE. "LAUNCE," one of the clowns, is the famous comedian WILL KEMPE. "LAUNCE'S" dog, CRAB is in KEMPE'S charge and is not helping much. There is no set. A helpful placard reading VERONA—AN OPEN PLACE, *is ready to hand. MUSICIANS can be heard tuning their instruments. From the other side of the curtain there is an expectant hubbub.*

KEMPE leads the dog into the wings and rummages in a box of props. He finds a skull. He has one foot on the box, his elbow on his knee, he looks at the skull . . . in other words he reminds us of Hamlet. We see this from the POV of WILL, who is just entering through a door backstage.

WILL

(approaching)

Prithee, Mr. Kempe, break a leg. You too, good Crab.

KEMPE

Crab is nervous. He has never played the Palace. When will you write me a tragedy, Will? I could do it.

WILL

No, they would laugh at Seneca if you played it.

WILL'S attention has been caught by ROSALINE, BURBAGE'S mistress. ROSALINE is big breasted, dark-eyed, dark-haired, sexual.

BURBAGE

(to ROSALINE)

My sleeve wants for a button, Mistress Rosaline, where were my seamstress's eyes?

BURBAGE kisses her mouth and slaps her behind. He comes over to greet WILL.

BURBAGE (Cont'd)

There is no dog in the first scene, Will Kempe, thank you. How goes it Will?

WILL

I am still owed money for this play, Burbage.

BURBAGE

Not from me. I only stole it. When are you coming over to the Chamberlain's Men?

WILL

When I have fifty pounds.

ROSALINE brings over the last elements of BURBAGE'S costume and helps him into them.

BURBAGE

Are you writing?

WILL

(nods somewhat defensively)

A comedy. All but done, a pirate comedy, wonderful.

BURBAGE

What is the chief part?

WILL

Romeo. Wit, swordsman, lover.

BURBAGE

The title?

WILL

Romeo.

BURBAGE

I will play him. Bring it tomorrow.

WILL

It's for Henslowe. He paid me.

BURBAGE

How much?

WILL

Ten pounds.

BURBAGE

You're a liar.

BURBAGE digs under his costume for his purse, which is on a waistband, over his corset.

WILL

I swear it. He wants *Romeo* for Ned and the Admiral's Men.

BURBAGE

Ned is wrong for it.

WILL turns to see HENSLOWE approaching.

BURBAGE (Cont'd)

(to WILL)

Here is two sovereigns—I'll give you two more when you show me the pages.

WILL

Done.

HENSLOWE

(arriving)

Burbage, I will see you hanged for a pickpocket.

BURBAGE

The Queen has commanded, she loves a comedy and the Master of the Revels favours us.

HENSLOWE

And what favour does Mr. Tilney receive from you?

BURBAGE

Ask him.

The Master of the Revels (TILNEY) comes through the curtain officiously.

TILNEY

She comes!

He disappears back through the curtains. The hubbub falls silent, rather dramatically, and all the busy PLAYERS know what that means: they all crowd to the curtain and find places to peep through.

INT. WHITEHALL PALACE. BANQUETING HALL. FRONT OF HOUSE/STAGE. DAY.

THE POV OF THE PLAYERS.

The arrival of QUEEN ELIZABETH, aged sixty, coming to take her place in the audience at front centre. The hall is crowded with lords and ladies, bowing ELIZABETH to her seat, which is raised high on a pedestal, affording the QUEEN an uninterrupted view of the play, and the audience an uninterrupted view of the QUEEN. Trumpets sound.

Close on a small piece of paper: a quill is writing "W. Shakespeare." WILL rolls the paper up carefully and slips it into the mouth of the snake bangle.

The curtain draws back and CONDELL as "VALENTINE" and BURBAGE as "PROTEUS" begin the play.

CONDELL AS VALENTINE

"Cease to persuade, my loving Proteus;
Home-keeping youth have ever homely wits . . . "

INT. WHITEHALL PALACE. BANQUETING HALL. THE WINGS/BACKSTAGE. DAY.

With BURBAGES'S presence accounted for on stage, ROSALINE curls an arm around WILL'S neck. They kiss hungrily. After a moment, WILL pulls back.

ROSALINE

When will you write me a sonnet, Will?

WILL

I have lost my gift.

ROSALINE

You left it in my bed. Come to look for it again.

WILL

Are you to be my muse, Rosaline?

ROSALINE

Burbage has my keeping but you have my heart.

WILL takes the snake bracelet and slips it onto her arm. ROSALINE looks at it, then at WILL. Then they kiss again, but WILL is distracted by the sound of coughing from the auditorium.

WILL

You see? The consumptives plot against me. "Will Shakespeare has a play, let us go and cough through it."

INT. WHITEHALL PALACE. BANQUETING HALL. STAGE. DAY.

"VALENTINE" is on stage with "PROTEUS."

CONDELL AS VALENTINE

"To be in love, where scorn is bought with groans;
Coy looks with heart sore sighs; One
fading moment's mirth
With twenty watchful, weary, tedious nights . . ."

As the scene continues, WILL appears at the back of the hall and finds himself next to HENSLOWE.

WILL

I feel a scene coming on.

HENSLOWE

Is it about a pirate's daughter?

INT. WHITEHALL PALACE. BACK OF THE BANQUETING HALL/STAGE. DAY.

Laughter.

It is later, and KEMPE is now on stage with his dog. The audience is roaring.

HENSLOWE

You see? Comedy.

QUEEN ELIZABETH'S idiosyncratic laugh rises above the others.

QUEEN

Well played, Master Crab, I commend you.

She throws a sweetmeat on the stage and the dog wolfs it down. Everyone applauds.

HENSLOWE

Love and a bit with a dog, that's what they like.

Now we meet VIOLA. VIOLA DE LESSEPS is twenty-five and beautiful, and she is laughing with great natural enjoyment. She sits slightly apart from her small family group—her parents, SIR ROBERT DE LESSEPS and LADY MARGARET DE LESSEPS. Part of the group but seated behind as befits her lower status is VIOLA'S NURSE.

Elsewhere is LORD WESSEX, our villain. WESSEX is in his forties, dark, cruel, self-important. He has noticed VIOLA. The nurse notices him.

VIOLA'S attention has been caught by WILL, standing lost in thought at the back of the hall.

INT. WHITEHALL PALACE. BANQUETING HALL. FRONT OF HOUSE/STAGE. DAY.

LATER.

"VALENTINE" is on stage alone. He is speaking the speech rather more coarsely than the version we hear later.

CONDELL AS VALENTINE

"What light is light if Silvia be not seen?
What joy is joy, if Silvia be not by?
Unless it be to think that she is by
And feed upon the shadow of perfection . . ."

Now we see that VIOLA knows the speech by heart, and is silently mouthing it with the actor.

HENSLOWE

There's a lady knows your play by heart.

But when he turns to WILL he finds that WILL has gone.

INT. WILL'S ROOM. DAY.

WILL comes into his room, goes straight to his table in the window, and arranges pen, ink, and paper.

Now he has his ritual: he spins round once in a circle, rubs his hands together and spits on the floor. Then he sits down, picks up his pen, and stares in front of him.

PAUSE.

Then he begins to write.

INT. DE LESSEPSES' HOUSE. VIOLA'S BEDROOM. NIGHT.

The NURSE is undressing her, though VIOLA tries intermittently to push her away. She is still bright with excitement.

VIOLA

Did you like Proteus or Valentine best? Proteus for speaking, Valentine for looks.

NURSE

I liked the dog, for laughs.

VIOLA

But Silvia I did not care for much. His fingers were red from fighting and he spoke like a schoolboy at lessons. Stage love will never be true love while the law of the land has our heroines played by pipsqueak boys in petticoats! Oh, when can we see another?

NURSE

When the Queen commands it.

VIOLA

But at the playhouse. Nurse?

NURSE

Be still.

Now the NURSE is cleaning VIOLA'S ears, one by one, of course. She has an ear-cleaning implement for this. VIOLA submits.

NURSE (Cont'd)

Playhouses are not for well-born ladies.

VIOLA

I am not so well-born.

NURSE

Well-monied is the same as well-born and well-married is more so. Lord Wessex was looking at you tonight.

VIOLA

All the men at court are without poetry. If they look at me they see my father's fortune. I will have poetry in my life. And adventure. And love. Love above all.

NURSE

Like Valentine and Silvia?

VIOLA

No . . . not the artful postures of love, but love that overthrows life. Unbiddable, ungovernable, like a riot in the heart, and nothing to be done, come ruin or rapture. Love like there has never been in a play.

(beat)

I will have love or I will end my days as a . . .

NURSE

As a nurse.

VIOLA

(kissing her)

But I would be Valentine and Silvia too. Good Nurse, God save you and good night. I would stay asleep my whole life if I could dream myself into a company of players.

VIOLA goes over to the window.

INT. DE LESSEPSES' HOUSE. VIOLA'S BEDROOM. NIGHT.

The NURSE thrusts a twig to her face.

NURSE

Clean your teeth while you dream, then.

Automatically, VIOLA takes the twig and begins brushing her teeth, all the while looking downriver towards the Rose. The NURSE attends her with a beaker of water, and a bowl.

NURSE (Cont'd)

Now spit . . .

VIOLA gazes longingly towards the Rose . . . And, there and then, she makes a plan.

EXT. SQUARE IN FRONT OF THE ROSE THEATRE. DAY.

HENSLOWE is making his way from the theatre to the market place when FENNYMAN and LAMBERT appear at either shoulder and propel him back the way he came. FREES follows behind.

FENNYMAN

This time we take your boots off!

HENSLOWE

What have I done, Mr. Fennyman?

FENNYMAN

The theatres are all closed by the plague!

HENSLOWE

Oh, that.

FENNYMAN

—by order of the Master of the Revels!

HENSLOWE

Mr. Fennyman, let me explain about the theatre business.

(they stop)

The natural condition is one of insurmountable obstacles on the road to imminent disaster. Believe me, to be closed by the plague is a bagatelle in the ups and downs of owning a theatre.

FENNYMAN

So what do we do?

HENSLOWE

Nothing. Strangely enough, it all turns out well.

FENNYMAN

How?

HENSLOWE

I don't know. It's a mystery.

LAMBERT

(dumbly)

Should I kill him, Mr. Fennyman?

At this point a rising din is heard in the background. A messenger, ringing a bell, is running through the street.

MESSENGER

. . . The theatres are reopened. By order of the Master of the Revels, the theatres are reopened . . . .

FENNYMAN is intrigued.

FREES

Mr. Fennyman! Mr. Tilney has opened the playhouses.

FENNYMAN

Yes I heard.

HENSLOWE plays his temporary advantage modestly, shrugging himself free of LAMBERT'S grip.

HENSLOWE
(*to LAMBERT*)

If you wouldn't mind . . .

HENSLOWE continues on his way. FENNYMAN watches HENSLOWE, curious.

FENNYMAN

Where is the play?

HENSLOWE

Oh, it's coming, it's coming.

INT. WILL'S ROOM. DAY.

It is. WILL is writing furiously. A burnt-down candle is still alight, although it is day outside the window. He has been writing all night. He has written about ten pages. Pleased with himself and excited, he gathers them up and leaves the room like a man with a mission.

EXT. WILL'S HOUSE. DAY.

Leaving the house, pages in hand, WILL nearly knocks down HENSLOWE who has come to see him.

HENSLOWE

Will! The theatres are . . .

Before he can finish, WILL brandishes the pages in his hand.

WILL

Romeo and Rosaline. Scene One! God, I'm good!

HENSLOWE

Rosaline? You mean Ethel.

WILL has gone.

EXT. BURBAGE'S HOUSE. DAY.

BURBAGE lives in another part of the city. WILL bangs through the door without ceremony.

WILL
(shouting)

Richard!

INT. BURBAGE'S HOUSE. DAY.

WILL enters and calls out.

WILL

Burbage?

INT. BURBAGE'S BEDROOM. DAY.

WILL charges into the bedroom. ROSALINE is in bed. The Master of the Revels is pulling up his breeches. WILL is shattered.

WILL

Mr. Tilney . . .

The unsuccessful snake bracelet glints at him from ROSALINE'S arm.

TILNEY

Like you, I found him not at home!

WILL

So this is the favour you find in the Chamberlain's Men.

ROSALINE

Will!

WILL

(to ROSALINE)

I would have made you immortal.

(turning to go)

Tell Burbage he has lost a new play by Will Shakespeare.

TILNEY

What does Burbage care of that? He is readying the Curtain for Kit Marlowe.

WILL

You have opened the playhouses?

TILNEY

I have, Master Shakespeare.

WILL

But the plague . . .

TILNEY

(sighs)

Yes, I know. But he was always hanging around the house.

A bell can be heard ringing outside.

ROSALINE

(to WILL, leaving)

Will . . . you're the only one, Will!—in my heart.

EXT. STREET. OUTSIDE BURBAGE'S HOUSE. DAY.

WILL emerges looking distraught.

A burning brazier stands by the wall. WILL thrusts the pages into the coals. He watches for a moment as the pages catch fire.

INT. TAVERN. DAY.

WILL walks in to find the place in an uproar of celebration. A handsome young serving man (NOL) is bumping through with a tray of tankards.

NOL

(excitedly)

Mr. Henslowe!

HENSLOWE

Yes, I heard. The theatres are open. But where is my playwright?

HENSLOWE finds a seat, and takes a tankard off NOL'S tray.

HENSLOWE

Chalk it up, Nol. I'm hungry, too.

NOL

The special today is a pig's foot marinated in juniper-berry vinegar, served with a buckwheat pancake which has been—

They are interrupted by WILL who joins them. He looks distracted.

HENSLOWE

Will! Have you finished?

WILL

Yes. Nearly.

(he taps his forehead)

It's all locked safe in here. We need Ralph for the Pirate King. Good morning, Master Nol. You will have a nice little part.

NOL shouts for joy, takes off his apron and flings it behind the bar. HENSLOWE jumps up and embraces WILL. The entire staff and half the customers are now crowding around, actors the lot of them. HENSLOWE bangs the table to shut them all up.

HENSLOWE

Ned Alleyn and the Admiral's Men are out on tour. I need actors. Those here who are unknown will have a chance to be known.

ACTOR

What about the money, Mr. Henslowe?

HENSLOWE

It won't cost you a penny! Auditions in half-an-hour!

The din of excited chatter returns. He sweeps grandly to the tavern door . . . where he meets RALPH BASHFORD, *a big, burly, middle-aged actor.*

HENSLOWE (Cont'd)

Ralph Bashford! I'd have a part for you but, alas, I hear you are a drunkard's drunkard.

RALPH

Never when I'm working!

INT. TAVERN. DAY.

WILL has remained behind, aghast now at his predicament. He goes to the bar.

WILL

Give me to drink mandragora.

BARMAN

Straight up, Will?

VOICE

Give my friend a beaker of your best brandy.

WILL turns towards a figure further down the bar. It's CHRISTOPHER MARLOWE.

WILL

Kit . . .

MARLOWE

How goes it, Will?

WILL

Wonderful, wonderful.

MARLOWE

Burbage says you have a play.

WILL

I have. And chinks to show for it.

His drink arrives. WILL places a sovereign on the bar.

WILL (Cont'd)

I insist—and a beaker for Mr. Marlowe.

The BARMAN does the business.

WILL (Cont'd)

I hear you have a new play for the Curtain.

MARLOWE

Not new—my *Doctor Faustus.*

WILL

I love your early work. "Was this the face that launched a thousand ships and burnt the topless towers of Ilium?"

MARLOWE

I have a new one nearly done, and better. *The Massacre at Paris.*

WILL

Good title.

MARLOWE

And yours?

WILL

Romeo and Ethel the Pirate's Daughter.

(beat; sighs despondently)

Yes, I know.

MARLOWE

What is the story?

WILL

Well, there's a pirate . . .

(confesses)

In truth, I have not written a word.

MARLOWE

Romeo is . . . Italian. Always in and out of love.

WILL

Yes, that's good. Until he meets . . .

MARLOWE

Ethel.

WILL

Do you think?

MARLOWE

The daughter of his enemy.

WILL

(thoughtfully)

The daughter of his enemy.

MARLOWE

His best friend is killed in a duel by Ethel's brother or something. His name is Mercutio.

WILL

Mercutio . . . good name.

NOL hurries back to WILL'S side.

NOL

Will—they're waiting for you!

WILL

I'm coming.

He drains his glass.

WILL (Cont'd)

Good luck with yours, Kit.

MARLOWE

I thought your play was for Burbage.

WILL

This is a different one.

MARLOWE

(trying to work it out)

A different one you haven't written?

WILL makes a helpless gesture and hurries after NOL.

INT. THE ROSE THEATRE. GALLERY/STAGE/ AUDITORIUM. DAY.

HENSLOWE and WILL are sitting in the gallery, listening to a YOUNG ACTOR auditioning.

YOUNG ACTOR

" . . . Was this the face that launched a thousand ships,
And burnt the topless towers of Ilium?
Sweet Helen, make me immortal with a kiss!"

HENSLOWE

Thank you!

HENSLOWE and WILL look a bit deflated. The YOUNG ACTOR leaves and is replaced by a SECOND ACTOR.

SECOND ACTOR

I would like to give you something from *Faustus* by Christopher Marlowe.

HENSLOWE

How refreshing.

SECOND ACTOR

"Was this the face that launched a thousand ships,
And burnt the topless towers of Ilium?"

HENSLOWE and WILL let him continue a bit further, but exchange despairing looks.

A succession of would-be actors offer their version of Marlowe's lines, each as inappropriate as the other. Among them is a small URCHIN.

URCHIN

" . . . the topless towers of Ilium?
Sweet Helen, make me immoral with a—!"

HENSLOWE

(bellows)

Thank you!

The URCHIN leaves, glowering furiously, and is replaced by a beanpole of a man (WABASH). WABASH has a bad stutter.

WABASH

"W-w-w-w-was th-th-this th-th-the f-f-f-face . . . "

HENSLOWE

(unexpectedly)

Very good, Mr. Wabash. Excellent. Report to the property master.

WILL looks at HENSLOWE in outrage.

HENSLOWE (Cont'd)

(apologetically)

My tailor. Wants to be an actor. I have a few debts here and there. Well, that seems to be everybody. Did you see a Romeo?

WILL

I did not.

HENSLOWE

Well, I to my work, you to yours. When can I see the pages?

WILL

Tomorrow . . .

HENSLOWE leaves him.

WILL (Cont'd)

(a prayer)

. . . please God.

WILL sits brooding alone for a moment. Then he realizes he is being addressed from the stage. ANOTHER ACTOR.

ACTOR

May I begin, sir?

WILL looks at the stage and sees a handsome young man, with a hat shadowing his eyes.

WILL

Your name?

VIOLA AS THOMAS

Thomas Kent. I would like to do a speech by a writer who commands the heart of every player.

WILL can hardly manage a nod.

VIOLA AS THOMAS (Cont'd)

"What light is light, if Silvia be not seen?
What joy is joy, if Silvia be not by? . . .
Unless it be to think that she is by
And feed upon the shadow of perfection.

It does not take four lines of "VALENTINE'S" speech to confirm for us, if confirmation be needed, that THOMAS is VIOLA. For WILL, amazement at hearing his own words soon gives way to something else. He is captivated. He has found his "ROMEO".

VIOLA AS THOMAS (Cont'd)

" . . . except I be by Silvia in the night,
There is no music in the nightingale.
Unless I look on Silvia in the day,
There is no day for me to look upon."

WILL interrupts "him."

WILL

Take off your hat.

VIOLA AS THOMAS

My hat?

WILL

Where did you learn how to do that?

VIOLA AS THOMAS

I . . .

WILL

Wait there.

VIOLA AS THOMAS

Are you Mr. Shakespeare?

WILL

Let me see you. Take off your hat.

THOMAS begins to panic. WILL jumps down to ground level. THOMAS runs offstage, to WILL'S bewilderment. WILL hurries after him. We go with WILL as he crosses the stage, then backstage, then into the . . .

INT. THE ROSE THEATRE. RETIRING ROOM. DAY.

. . . RETIRING ROOM which is crowded with actors and HENSLOWE'S lieutenant, property manager, copier, and general factotum who is a new character, PETER.

ACTOR

What are we playing?

NOL

Where are the pages?

WILL enters into the middle of this.

WILL

(shouts)

Where's the boy?

NOBODY knows what he is talking about. WABASH, the stutterer, grabs Will's hand and shakes it excitedly.

WABASH

B-b-b-b-break a l-l-l-leg!

The street door is swinging shut. WILL sees it. He fights his way through the men to get to the door.

EXT. THE ROSE THEATRE. BANKSIDE. DAY.

WILL emerges from the theatre into a street throbbing with nefarious life. Whores, cutpurses, hawkers, urchins, tract-sellers, riffraff of all kinds in an area of stews (lowdown pubs), brothels and slums. It is some time before WILL spots THOMAS, way ahead of him in the crowded street. The chase is taking them to the riverbank.

EXT. THE RIVER. DAY.

When WILL gets to the riverbank he sees that THOMAS is in a smallish boat being rowed upriver and in midstream. The river is quite busy, and among the boats there are a number of waiting "taxis." WILL jumps into the nearest one and shouts at the "Taxi Driver" BOATMAN.

WILL

Follow that boat!

BOATMAN

Right you are, governor!

WILL sits in the stern of the boat and the BOATMAN sits facing him, rowing lustily.

BOATMAN (Cont'd)

I know your face. Are you an actor?

WILL

(oh God, here we go again)

Yes.

BOATMAN

Yes, I've seen you in something. That one about a king.

WILL

Really?

BOATMAN

I had that Christopher Marlowe in my boat once.

EXT. THE RIVER. DAY.

LATER.

The BOATMAN is puffing. WILL is looking ahead to where THOMAS'S boat has reached a jetty on the farther shore, a private jetty attached to a rich house on the north bank. WILL sees THOMAS jump out of his boat and run toward the house.

WILL

Do you know that house?

BOATMAN

Sir Robert De Lesseps.

EXT. DE LESSEPSES' HOUSE. DAY.

WILL runs towards the house.

INT. DE LESSEPSES' HOUSE. DAY.

THOMAS rushes up the back stairs, removing his hat. Her hair tumbles down about her shoulders, so we will call her VIOLA again.

INT. DE LESSEPSES' HOUSE. VIOLA'S BEDROOM. DAY.

Her mother, LADY DE LESSEPS, is talking to the NURSE.

LADY DE LESSEPS

Where is she? Our guests are upon us, Lord Wessex too, bargaining for a bride. My husband will have it settled tonight.

Behind her, the door opens revealing VIOLA as THOMAS to the NURSE'S view, but only for a moment. The door closes again as LADY DE LESSEPS turns.

LADY DE LESSEPS (Cont'd)

Tomorrow he drags me off to the country and it will be three weeks gone before we return from our estates.

A different door communicating to the next room, opens and VIOLA comes in after a lightning dress change into a robe. She curtseys to her mother.

VIOLA

God save you, mother.

(to NURSE)

Hot water, nurse.

The NURSE looks at her, round-eyed.

INT. DE LESSEPSES' HOUSE. KITCHEN. DAY.

From a cauldron on the stove, hot water is poured intotwo pails, by a KITCHEN BOY under the NURSE'S command.

SCULLERY MAID (O.S.)

Thomas Kent, sir? No sir.

WILL (O.S.)

The actor.

NURSE

Who asks for him?

WILL has come to the kitchen door with a letter.

WILL

William Shakespeare, actor, poet, and playwright of the Rose.

The NURSE sends the SCULLERY MAID back to work.

NURSE

Master Kent is . . . my nephew.

WILL

(giving her the letter)

I will wait.

NURSE

Much good may it do you.

INT. DE LESSEPSES' HOUSE. VIOLA'S BATHROOM. EVENING.

VIOLA in her bath, reads WILL'S letter. The NURSE is adding hot water to the tub.

VIOLA

(delighted)

He sees himself in me! Romeo Montague, a young man of Verona!

NURSE

(unimpressed)

Verona again.

VIOLA

(devouring the letter)

A comedy of quarrelling families reconciled in the discovery of Romeo to be the very same Capulet cousin stolen from the cradle and fostered to manhood by his Montague mother that was robbed of her own child by the Pirate King!

EXT. DE LESSEPSES' HOUSE. NIGHT.

WILL waits hopefully. The kitchen door opens and a SERVANT flings a bucket of dirty water in the general direction of the gutter. WILL hops nimbly aside and escapes a soaking.

SERVANT

Be off!

INT. DE LESSEPSES' HOUSE. VIOLA'S BEDROOM. NIGHT.

The NURSE is helping VIOLA into her party dress.

NURSE

Your mother, and your father—

VIOLA

(gaily)

From tomorrow, away in the country for three weeks! Is Master Shakespeare not handsome?

NURSE

He looks well enough for a mountebank.

VIOLA

Oh, Nurse! He would give Thomas Kent the life of Viola De Lesseps's dreaming.

NURSE

(firmly)

My lady, this play will end badly. I will tell.

VIOLA

(twice as firmly)

You will not tell. As you love me and as I love you, you will bind my breast and buy me a boy's wig!

EXT. DE LESSEPSES' HOUSE. NIGHT.

WILL spots a gaggle of MUSICIANS approaching, carrying instruments. WILL recognizes them.

WILL

Master Plum! What business here?

MUSICIAN

A five shilling business, Will. We play for the dancing.

The sound of hooves gives hardly any warning as a GALLOPING HORSEMAN thunders through the MUSICIANS who have to leap out of the way. It is WESSEX arriving at the house, with his usual good manners. Will watches WESSEX skid to a halt and enter the house.

INT. DE LESSEPSES' HOUSE. BANQUETING ROOM. NIGHT.

WILL has got in with the MUSICIANS. Competently enough he strums along with them on the bandstand. Two dozen guests are enough to crowd the space for dancing. WILL glances around, looking for THOMAS KENT.

He stops a passing SERVANT, helping himself to a snack off the man's tray.

SERVANT

Musicians don't eat, Sir Robert's orders.

WILL

I seek Master Thomas Kent.

It means nothing to the SERVANT who moves on.

ANGLE ON WESSEX and SIR ROBERT.

SIR ROBERT

She is a beauty, my lord, as would take a king to church for a dowry of a nutmeg.

WESSEX

My plantations in Virginia are not mortgaged for a nutmeg. I have an ancient name that will bring you preferment when your grandson is a Wessex. Is she fertile?

SIR ROBERT

She will breed. If she do not, send her back.

WESSEX

Is she obedient?

SIR ROBERT

As any mule in Christendom. But if you are the man to ride her, there are rubies in the saddlebag.

WESSEX

I like her.

ANGLE on WILL—watching the dancing. Then he sees VIOLA in the crowd. He turns to blood. Love at first sight, no doubt about it. VIOLA has not seen him. She is doing a daughter's duty among her parents' friends. The guests form up to begin a changing-partners dance (the very same one you get in every ROMEO and JULIET).

WILL

(to Musician)

By all the stars in heaven, who is she?

MUSICIAN

Viola de Lesseps. Dream on, Will.

WILL leaves the bandstand and is moving trancelike to keep her in view between the dancers and onlookers.

VIOLA moves through the patterns of the dance until . . . as night follows day, she finds WILL opposite her. He has insinuated himself into the dance. VIOLA gasps.

VIOLA

Master Shakespeare . . .

WILL reacts, surprised by her reaction.

The dance separates them.

VIOLA finds herself opposite WESSEX.

WESSEX

My lady Viola.

VIOLA

My lord.

WESSEX

I have spoken with your father.

VIOLA

So, my lord? I speak with him every day.

WESSEX scowls. The dance separates them. VIOLA finds herself opposite WILL again. WILL stares at her entranced.

VIOLA (Cont'd)

Good sir . . . ?

WILL has lost his tongue

VIOLA (Cont'd)

I heard you are a poet.

WILL nods in his trance and she smiles at him.

VIOLA (Cont'd)

But a poet of no words?

WILL tries to speak but the silver tongue won't work. He is dumb with adoration.

Suddenly WESSEX takes him affably by the elbow and leads him into an alcove.

WESSEX

(smiling evilly)

"Poet?"

WILL

(coming round from the anaesthetic and not noticing the danger)

I was a poet till now, but I have seen beauty that puts my poems at one with the talking ravens at the Tower.

To his surprise he finds a lordly dagger at his throat.

WILL (Cont'd)

(startled)

How do I offend, my lord?

WESSEX

By coveting my property. I cannot shed blood in her house but I will cut your throat anon. You have a name?

WILL

(gulps)

Christopher Marlowe at your service.

WESSEX shoves him through the nearest door.

VIOLA'S eyes are searching the room for WILL. She finds WESSEX smiling at her. She looks away.

EXT. DE LESSEPS' GARDEN/VIOLA'S BALCONY. NIGHT.

There is a lighted window on the balcony. VIOLA, dressed for bed, and the NURSE pass across the lighted space.

WILL is in the garden. He sees her. The light in the room is extinguished. WILL sighs. Then VIOLA comes out onto the balcony in the moonlight. WILL gasps. He watches her. VIOLA sighs dreamily.

VIOLA

Romeo, Romeo . . . a young man of Verona. A comedy. By William Shakespeare.

WILL reckons that's a good enough cue. He comes out of hiding, and approaches the balcony.

WILL

(whispers)

My lady!

VIOLA

(gasps)

Who is there?

WILL

Will Shakespeare!

The NURSE calls "Madam!" from inside the room.

VIOLA

Anon, good nurse. Anon.

(to Will)

Master Shakespeare?!

WILL

The same, alas.

VIOLA

Oh but why "alas?"

WILL

A lowly player.

VIOLA

Alas indeed, for I thought you the highest poet of my esteem and a writer of plays that capture my heart.

WILL

Oh—I am him too!

The NURSE calls again.

VIOLA

(to NURSE)

Anon, anon!

(to WILL)

I will come again.

She goes inside for a moment.

WILL

(to himself)

Oh, I am fortune's fool, I will be punished for this!

VIOLA returns. WILL comes forward again.

WILL (Cont'd)

Oh my lady, my love!

VIOLA

If they find you here they will kill you.

WILL

You can bring them with a word.

VIOLA

Oh, not for the world!

The NURSE calls her again: "Madam!"

VIOLA (Cont'd)

Anon, nurse!

But she goes inside. WILL looks around and sees that there is, as ever, a convenient tree. He starts to climb up toward the balcony. When his head is nearly level, a soft figure comes once more onto the balcony. WILL pops his head over the parapet and is face to face with the NURSE. The NURSE gives a yell. WILL falls out of the tree

EXT. DE LESSEPSES' HOUSE. NIGHT.

Male voices shout to each other inside the house, candle flames appear in different windows, the garden door is flung open, revealing SIR ROBERT with candelabra in one hand and sword in the other.

By this time WILL is on top of the garden wall and he drops safely out of sight. He could have written it better.

INT. WILL'S ROOM. DAWN.

WILL is burning the midnight oil—literally and metaphorically. His quill has already covered a dozen sheets. He is inspired.

INT. THE ROSE THEATRE. STAGE/AUDITORIUM. DAY.

It is day one. THE COMPANY is on stage. PETER is passing pages around a bunch of actors. JOHN, JAMES, and NOL are looking through their pages.

JOHN

"Draw if you be men!

(to JAMES)

Gregory, remember thy washing blow."

NOL

"Part, fools, put up your swords."

WILL is going around pumping hands and slapping shoulders, flushed with excitement.

HENSLOWE is reading his pages, worried. RALPH BASHFORD is next to him.

HENSLOWE

It starts well, and then it's all long-faced about some Rosaline. Where's the comedy, Will. Where's the dog?

(to RALPH)

Do you think it is funny?

RALPH

I was a Pirate King, now I'm a Nurse. That's funny.

WILL pulls HENSLOWE aside.

WILL

We are at least six men short, and those we have will be overparted, ranters and stutterers who should be sent back to the stews. My Romeo has let me down. I see disaster.

HENSLOWE

We are at least four acts short, Will, if you are looking for disaster.

WILL notices a young scruffy thirteen-year-old actor, the URCHIN we met before.

WILL

Who are you, master?

URCHIN

I am Ethel, sir, the Pirate's daughter.

WILL

(furiously)

I'll be damned if you are!

And he helps the URCHIN off with a kick. The URCHIN glowers with resentment. HENSLOWE finds himself face to face with FENNYMAN.

FENNYMAN

Is it going well?

HENSLOWE

Very well.

FENNYMAN

But nothing is happening.

HENSLOWE

Yes, but very well.

WILL

(shouts)

Gentlemen! Thank you! You are welcome.

FENNYMAN

Who is that?

HENSLOWE

Nobody. The author.

WILL

We are about to embark on a great voyage.

HENSLOWE

It is customary to make a little speech on the first day. It does no harm and authors like it.

WILL

You want to know what parts you are to receive. All will be settled as we go—

FENNYMAN

I'll do it.

(he jumps on the stage and takes over)

Listen to me, you dregs!—actors are ten a penny, and I, Hugh Fennyman, hold your nuts in my hand—

That's as far as he gets before there is a dramatic interruption—the public entrance door is flung open and SIX MEN make a loud entrance, headed by NED ALLEYN, the actor, who is a handsome piratical figure with a big voice and a big sword.

ALLEYN

Huzzah! The Admiral's Men are returned to the house!

He gets various reactions. HENSLOWE and WILL shout his name joyfully; some of the actors are friends with the new group and behave accordingly, others know they are out of a job. FENNYMAN recovers, or tries to.

FENNYMAN

Who is this?

ALLEYN slaps him aside with his sword.

ALLEYN

(roars)

Silence, you dog! I am Hieronimo! I am Tamburlaine! I am Faustus! I am Barrabas, the Jew of Malta—oh yes, Master Will, and I am Henry VI. What is the play, and what is my part?

FENNYMAN is impressed.

FENNYMAN

A moment, sir!

ALLEYN

(roars)

Who are you?

FENNYMAN

(bleating)

I am the money!

ALLEYN

Then you may remain so long as you remain silent. Pay attention and you will see how genius creates a legend.

FENNYMAN

(respectfully)

Thank you, sir.

WILL

We are in desperate want of a Mercutio, Ned, a young nobleman of Verona . . .

ALLEYN

And the title of this piece?

WILL

Mercutio.

HENSLOWE

Is it?

ALLEYN

I will play him!

Half a dozen of the ADMIRAL'S MEN will be given roles in our play and we meet them and identify them as Will enthusiastically shakes hands.

WILL

Mr. Pope! Mr. Philips! Welcome, George Bryan! James Armitage!
(and now greeting SAM GOSSE, the female star of the Admiral's Men)
Sam! My pretty one! Are you ready to fall in love again?

SAM
(hoarsely)

I am, Master Shakespeare.

WILL
(concerned)

But your voice . . .
(he thrusts a hand between SAM'S legs)
Have they dropped?

SAM
(a girlier voice now)

No, no, a touch of cold only.

We suspect he is lying but WILL has turned away.

WILL

Master Henslowe, you have your actors.

He leaves, passing by the humbled FENNYMAN.

FENNYMAN

I saw his Tamburlaine, you know. Wonderful.

WILL

Yes, I saw it.

FENNYMAN

Of course, it was mighty writing. There is no one like Marlowe.

WILL is used to it. He goes.

EXT. RIVERBANK. DAY.

WILL arrives in a hurry at the wharfside, and looks vainly in the direction of the DE LESSEPSES' house: no THOMAS.

EXT. THE ROSE THEATRE. STAGE DOOR. DAY.

WILL looks down the alley:—no THOMAS. He turns away. The URCHIN, the short-lived Ethel, is sitting in the alley.

WILL

Better fortune, boy.

URCHIN

(shrugs)

I was in a play. They cut my head off in *Titus Andronicus*. When I write plays, they will be like *Titus*.

WILL

(pleased)

You admire it?

The URCHIN nods grimly.

URCHIN

I liked it when they cut heads off. And the daughter mutilated with knives.

WILL

Oh. What is your name?

URCHIN

John Webster. Here, kitty, kitty.

Because a stray cat is nearby. The cat shows an interest. The URCHIN passes a white mouse to the cat and watches the result with sober interest.

URCHIN (Cont'd)

Plenty of blood. That is the only writing.

WILL backs away, unnerved by the boy.

URCHIN (Cont'd)

Wait, you'll see the cat bites his head off.

WILL

I have to get back.

INT. THE ROSE THEATRE. STAGE/AUDITORIUM. DAY.

On stage . . . the actors carry their parts.

NOL AS BENVOLIO

"See where he comes. So please you step aside;
I'll know his grievance or be much denied."

MONTAGUE

"I would thou wert so happy by thy stay
To hear true shrift. Come, madam, let's away."

Onstage "MONTAGUE" and "LADY MONTAGUE" make their exit. Offstage, WILL appears next to HENSLOWE.

WILL

Cut round him for now.

HENSLOWE

(not understanding)

What? Who?

WILL

Romeo.

HENSLOWE

The one who came with your letter?

WILL

What?

NOL AS BENVOLIO (O.S.)

"Good morrow, cousin."

VIOLA AS ROMEO (O.S.)

"Is the day so young?"

The voice is THOMAS'S. WILL turns back to the stage and sees him. Today THOMAS has a wig as well as his small moustache.

NOL AS BENVOLIO

"But new struck nine."

VIOLA AS ROMEO

"Ay me, sad hours seem long.
Was that my father that went hence so fast?"

NOL AS BENVOLIO

"It was. What sadness lengthens Romeo's hours?"

VIOLA AS ROMEO

"Not having that which, having, makes them short."

WILL

Good . . .

NOL AS BENVOLIO

"In love?"

VIOLA AS ROMEO

"Out."

NOL AS BENVOLIO

"Of love?"

VIOLA AS ROMEO

"Out of her favour where I am in love."

WILL

(interrupting)

No, no, no . . . Don't spend it all at once!

The rehearsal stops.

VIOLA AS THOMAS

Yes, sir.

WILL

Do you understand me?

VIOLA AS THOMAS

No, sir.

WILL

He is speaking about a baggage we never even meet! What will be left in your purse when he meets his Juliet?

HENSLOWE

Juliet? You mean Ethel.

WILL

(rounding on him)

God's teeth, am I to suffer this constant stream of interruption?!

(to THOMAS)

What will you do in Act Two when he meets the love of his life?

VIOLA AS THOMAS

(timidly—looking through his few sheets of paper)

I am very sorry, sir, I have not seen Act Two.

WILL

Of course you have not! I have not written it!

Alone in the auditorium, FENNYMAN looks and listens, fascinated. So this is theatre!

WILL (Cont'd)

Go once more!

NED ALLEYN comes out of the wings, frowning over his manuscript.

ALLEYN

Will . . . Where is Mercutio?

WILL

(tapping his forehead)

Locked safe in here. I leave the scene in your safe keeping, Ned, I have a sonnet to write.

WILL moves back into the wings where HENSLOWE is looking anxious.

HENSLOWE

A sonnet? You mean a play.

WILL moves on, ignoring him. As he goes, we see that VIOLA is love-struck by him, a riot in the heart.

INT. DE LESSEPSES' HOUSE. STAIRCASE. DAY.

VIOLA still dressed as THOMAS, sonnet in hand, runs up the stairs to her room. From the other end of the house WESSEX can be heard ranting.

INT. DE LESSEPSES' HOUSE. HALL. NIGHT.

LORD WESSEX is being kept waiting. The NURSE is bearing the brunt of his impatience.

WESSEX

Two hours at prayer!

NURSE

Lady Viola is pious, my lord.

WESSEX

Piety is for Sunday! And two hours at prayer is not piety, it is self-importance!

NURSE

It would be better that you return tomorrow, my lord.

WESSEX

It would be better that you tell her to get off her knees and show some civility to her six-day lord and master.

VIOLA opens the door. She has changed hurriedly—too hurriedly: the effect of her glorious hair falling to her bare shoulders is spoiled by her moustache. Fortunately, the NURSE spots her before WESSEX does and by coming forward to greet her, the NURSE manages to shield Viola from view, communicate the problem, and announce WESSEX'S presence, so that by the time the NURSE has passed by VIOLA and let herself out of the room, the moustache has disappeared.

WESSEX (Cont'd)

My lady Viola.

VIOLA

Lord Wessex. You have been waiting.

WESSEX

I am aware of it, but it is beauty's privilege.

VIOLA

You flatter, my lord.

WESSEX

No. I have spoken to the Queen.

(pause)

Her majesty's consent is requisite when a Wessex takes a wife, and once gained, her consent is her command.

VIOLA

Do you intend to marry, my lord?

WESSEX

Your father should keep you better informed. He has bought me for you. He returns from his estates to see us married two weeks from Saturday.

(pause)

You are allowed to show your pleasure.

VIOLA

I do not love you, my lord.

WESSEX

How your mind hops about! Your father was a shopkeeper, your children will bear arms, and I will recover my fortune. That is the only matter under discussion today. You will like Virginia.

VIOLA

Virginia?!

WESSEX

Why, yes! My fortune lies in my plantations. The tobacco weed. I need four thousand pounds to fit out a ship and put my investments to work—I fancy tobacco has a future. We will not stay there long, three or four years . . .

VIOLA

But why me?

WESSEX

It was your eyes. No, your lips.

He kisses her with more passion than ceremony. VIOLA recoils, and slaps him.

WESSEX (Cont'd)

Will you defy your father and your Queen?

VIOLA

The Queen has consented?

WESSEX

She wants to inspect you. At Greenwich,come Sunday. Be submissive, modest, grateful and brief.

VIOLA

(forced to submit)

I will do my duty, my lord.

INT. DE LESSEPSES' HOUSE. VIOLA'S BEDROOM. NIGHT.

She is writing to WILL. His letter-poem is on her table. We can read part of it: "Shall I compare thee to a summer's day . . . "

Now we see what VIOLA is writing.

INSERT: "Master Will, poet dearest to my heart, I beseech you, banish me from yours—I am to marry Lord Wessex—a daughter's duty . . . "

She sheds a romantic, unhappy tear.

INT. THE ROSE THEATRE. STAGE. DAY.

SAM is now "JULIET". The play has evidently reached Act I Scene 5. We are witnessing the meeting of "ROMEO" and "JULIET" in a simplified version of the changing-partners dance we saw at VIOLA'S house. NED ALLEYN is in charge.

ALLEYN

Gentlemen upstage, ladies downstage!

The dance goes wrong. It is THOMAS'S fault.

ALLEYN (Cont'd)

(furious)

Gentlemen upstage! Ladies downstage! Are you a lady, Mr. Kent?

THOMAS mutters a blushing apology. WILL arrives among the bystanders, clutching fresh pages. He gives these to PETER. NED ALLEYN sees him and comes over to start an argument.

WILL

(preempting)

You did not like the speech?

ALLEYN

The speech is excellent.

(he does the first line impressively)

"Oh then I see Queen Mab hath been with you!" Excellent and a good length. But then he disappears for the length of a bible.

WILL points significantly at the pages he has given PETER.

WILL

There you have his duel, a skirmish of words and swords such as I never wrote, nor anyone. He dies with such passion and poetry as you ever heard: "a plague on both your houses!"

NED nods satisfied and turns back to work. Then he turns back.

ALLEYN

He dies?

But the author has escaped.

INT. THE ROSE THEATRE. WRITER'S CORNER. DAY.

Up aloft, WILL has a Writer's Corner where he settles down to work. We see his private superstition: he spins round in a circle, rubs his hands together, and spits on the floor. That done, he picks up his pen.

EXT. STREET. NIGHT.

WILL is charging down a narrow alley, and bumps into BURBAGE who is emerging from the door of a tavern.

BURBAGE

Will!

WILL is in too much of a hurry to stop. BURBAGE calls after him.

BURBAGE (Cont'd)

And where are my pages . . .

WILL hurries on.

EXT. RIVERBANK. DUSK.

VIOLA as THOMAS is being rowed across the river. From behind, in the direction of Bankside, "he" hears shouting.

WILL

(O.S. shouting)

Did you give her my letter?

VIOLA as THOMAS turns to see WILL some way behind, following in another boat. She takes a letter from her coat and holds it aloft.

VIOLA AS THOMAS

(calling)

And this is for you.

EXT. THE RIVER. VIOLA'S BOAT. NIGHT.

WILL has climbed aboard VIOLA'S boat and is tearing open the letter. What he reads causes him great pain. He collapses into the stern seat next to VIOLA.

WILL

Oh, Thomas! She has cut my strings! I am unmanned, unmended, and unmade, like a puppet in a box.

BOATMAN

Writer, is he?

WILL turns on him savagely.

WILL

Row your boat.

EXT. THE RIVER. VIOLA'S BOAT. NIGHT.

WILL turns back to VIOLA. They have their conversation intimately, disregarding the lack of intimacy. The BOATMAN is hardly an arm's length away, but they ignore him.

WILL

She tells me to keep away. She is to marry Lord Wessex. What should I do?

VIOLA AS THOMAS

If you love her, you must do what she asks.

WILL

And break her heart and mine?

VIOLA AS THOMAS

It is only yours you can know.

WILL

She loves me, Thomas!

VIOLA AS THOMAS

Does she say so?

WILL

No. And yet she does where the ink has run with tears. Was she weeping when she gave you this?

VIOLA AS THOMAS

I . . . Her letter came to me by the nurse.

WILL

Your aunt?

VIOLA AS THOMAS

(catching up)

Yes, my aunt. But perhaps she wept a little. Tell me how you love her, Will.

WILL

Like a sickness and its cure together.

VIOLA AS THOMAS

Yes, like rain and sun, like cold and heat.

(collecting herself)

Is your lady beautiful? Since I came to visit from the country, I have not seen her close. Tell me, is she beautiful?

WILL

Oh, if I could write the beauty of her eyes! I was born to look in them and know myself.

He is looking into VIOLA'S eyes. She holds his look, but WILL belies his words.

VIOLA AS THOMAS

And her lips?

WILL

Oh, Thomas, her lips! The early morning rose would wither on the branch, if it could feel envy!

VIOLA AS THOMAS

And her voice? Like lark song?

WILL

Deeper. Softer. None of your twittering larks! I would banish nightingales from her garden before they interrupt her song.

VIOLA AS THOMAS

She sings too?

WILL

Constantly. Without doubt. And plays the lute, she has a natural ear. And her bosom—did I mention her bosom?

VIOLA AS THOMAS

(glinting)

What of her bosom?

WILL

Oh Thomas, a pair of pippins! As round and rare as golden apples!

VIOLA AS THOMAS

I think the lady is wise to keep your love at a distance. For what lady could live up to it close to, when her eyes and lips and voice may be no more beautiful than mine? Besides, can a lady born to wealth and noble marriage love happily with a Bankside poet and player?

WILL

(fervently)

Yes, by God! Love knows nothing of rank or riverbank! It will spark between a queen and the poor vagabond who plays the king, and their love should be minded by each, for love denied blights the soul we owe to God! So tell my lady, William Shakespeare waits for her in the garden!

VIOLA AS THOMAS

But what of Lord Wessex?

WILL

For one kiss, I would defy a thousand Wessexes!

The boat scrapes on the jetty of the DE LESSEPSES' house. The bump throws THOMAS into WILL'S arms. He holds her round the shoulders. His words have almost unmasked her. The closeness does the rest. She kisses him on the mouth and jumps out of the boat.

VIOLA

Oh, Will!

She throws a coin to the BOATMAN and runs towards the house.

BOATMAN

Thank you, my lady!

WILL

(stunned)

Lady?

BOATMAN

Viola De Lesseps. Known her since she was this high.
Wouldn't deceive a child.

WILL gets out of the boat.

BOATMAN (Cont'd)

(reaching under his seat)

Strangely enough, I'm a bit of a writer myself.

The BOATMAN produces his memoirs in manuscript.

BOATMAN (Cont'd)

It wouldn't take you long to read it, I expect you know all the booksellers . . .

But WILL has gone.

EXT. DE LESSEPSES' GARDEN. NIGHT.

WILL drops over the wall into the garden and without hesitation starts climbing up to her balcony.

INT. DE LESSEPSES' HOUSE. VIOLA'S BEDROOM. NIGHT.

WILL comes in through the window, just as VIOLA enters by the door. They stare at each other across the room.

WILL

Can you love a fool?

VIOLA

Can you love a player?

They run together and fall into a passionate kiss.

WILL

(springs back)

Wait! You are still a maid and perhaps as mistook in me as I was mistook in Thomas Kent.

VIOLA

Answer me only this: are you the author of the plays of William Shakespeare?

WILL

I am.

VIOLA

Then kiss me again for I am not mistook.

They run together and fall into a passionate kiss. VIOLA fumbles with his clothing, he with hers.

VIOLA (Cont'd)

I do not know how to undress a man.

WILL

It is strange to me, too.

INT. DE LESSEPSES' HOUSE. OUTSIDE VIOLA'S BEDROOM. NIGHT.

The NURSE has come to listen. She puts her ear against the door. Because she hears muffled voices, she looks startled.

INT. DE LESSEPSES' HOUSE. VIOLA'S BEDROOM. NIGHT.

WILL is half naked. VIOLA is down to her petticoat, and chemise. The petticoat comes away. WILL flings it aside. He takes off her chemise. He is startled to find that she is tightly bandaged round the bosom. WILL finds the loose end and spins her naked.

INT. DE LESSEPSES' HOUSE. OUTSIDE VIOLA'S BED-ROOM. NIGHT.

The NURSE, drags a chair—a rocker—outside the bedroom door, and takes up her position. She sits down, keeping guard. Pretty soon there comes the regular creak of VIOLA'S bed. The NURSE fans herself furiously with her little lacy fan. She crosses herself. A CHAMBERMAID comes along the gallery outside the bedroom door. She is dusting her way along. The CHAMBERMAID becomes aware of the regular creaking. She pauses. The NURSE begins to rock in her chair, keeping time with the creaking from within. The CHAMBERMAID stares at the NURSE. The NURSE stares at the CHAMBERMAID.

NURSE

Go to, go to.

INT. DE LESSEPSES' HOUSE. VIOLA'S BEDROOM. NIGHT.

WILL and VIOLA have finished making love, and lie in each other's arms.

VIOLA

I would not have thought it. There is something better than a play.

WILL

There is.

VIOLA

Even your play.

WILL

(frowns)

Oh . . .

VIOLA

And that was only my first try.

WILL

Well perhaps better than my first.

(he kisses her again)

EXT. DE LESSEPSES' HOUSE. DAWN.

Dawn is breaking. The sun is lacing the severing clouds with envious streaks.

INT. DE LESSEPSES' HOUSE. OUTSIDE VIOLA'S BEDROOM. DAWN.

The NURSE has fallen asleep in her rocking chair.

INT. DE LESSEPSES' HOUSE. VIOLA'S BEDROOM. DAWN.

A rooster crows at some distance. VIOLA and WILL are in bed. She stirs drowsily. VIOLA, coming awake, speaks his name and he kisses her.

VIOLA

Will . . .

Then he starts to get out of bed.

VIOLA (Cont'd)

You would not leave me?

WILL

I must. Look—how pale the window.

VIOLA

(pulling him down)

Moonlight!

WILL

No, the morning rooster woke me.

VIOLA

It was the owl—come to bed—

She is winning. She kisses him and pulls the bedclothes around them.

WILL

(giving in)

Oh, let Henslowe wait.

VIOLA

(pausing, pushing him away)

Mr. Henslowe?

WILL

(persisting)

Let him be damned for his pages!

VIOLA

Oh—no, no!

WILL

(kissing her)

There is time. It is still dark.

VIOLA

It is broad day!

(the rooster crows again)

The rooster tells us so!

WILL

It was the owl. Believe me, love, it was the owl.

He kisses her and starts to make love to her again. VIOLA gives him a shove which pushes him onto the floor. She sits up and pulls on her gown.

VIOLA

You would leave us players without a scene to read today?!

There's a knock at the door.

INT. DE LESSEPSES' HOUSE. CORRIDOR OUTSIDE VIOLA'S BEDROOM/VIOLA'S BEDROOM. DAWN.

The NURSE is knocking. VIOLA comes to the door.

NURSE

My lady, the house is stirring, it is a new day.

VIOLA looks beautified by the hours that have passed.

VIOLA

It is a new world!

INT. THE ROSE THEATRE. STAGE/AUDITORIUM. DAY.

The cut is to the middle of a rehearsal. We are coming up to the moment when "ROMEO" and "JULIET" kiss for the first time (Act I Scene V)

NED ALLEYN is in charge but WILL is watching. His life has turned perfect.

VIOLA AS ROMEO

" . . . Have not saints lips, and holy palmers too?"

SAM AS JULIET

"Ay pilgrim, lips that they must use in prayer."

VIOLA AS ROMEO

"Oh then, dear saint, let lips do what hands do:
They pray: grant thou, lest faith turn to despair."

WILL is in her eye-line. Her eyes flash an intimate secret look to him.

SAM AS JULIET

"Saints do not move, though grant for prayer's sake."

And VIOLA misses her cue as a result.

SAM
(prompting her)
It's you.

ALLEYN
(roars)
Suffering cats!

VIOLA guiltily picks up her line.

VIOLA AS ROMEO
"Then move not, while my prayer's effect I take."

In character, VIOLA kisses SAM, demurely, but apparently not demurely enough for WILL, who gives a twitch.

VIOLA AS ROMEO (Cont'd)
"Thus from my lips, by thine, my sin is purg'd."

SAM AS JULIET
"Then have my lips the sin that they have took."

VIOLA AS ROMEO
"Sin from my lips? Oh trespass sweetly urg'd.
Give me my sin again."

VIOLA kisses SAM again. WILL gives a major twitch, which in fact catapults his body onto the stage. Everybody looks at him in surprise.

WILL
Yes . . . yes . . . er . . . not quite right . . . it is more . . .
let me . . .
(as JULIET)
"Then have my lips the sin that they have took."

VIOLA AS ROMEO

"Sin from my lips? Oh trespass sweetly urg'd.
Give me my sin again."

VIOLA kisses WILL. They lose themselves for a fraction of a moment. As VIOLA withdraws her lips, WILL'S lips are going for it again.

VIOLA AS ROMEO (Cont'd)

"You kiss by th' book."

ALLEYN

(to Will, sarcastically)

Well! It was lucky you were here! Why do not I write the rest of your play while you—

WILL

(apologising, retreating)

Yes, yes . . . continue. Now the Nurse. Where is Ralph?

RALPH has been ready and waiting.

RALPH AS NURSE

"Madam, your mother craves a word with you."

VIOLA AS ROMEO

"What is her mother?"

RALPH AS NURSE

"Marry bachelor, Her mother is the lady of the house . . . "

WILL has retreated to . . .

INT. THE ROSE THEATRE. BACKSTAGE. DAY.

He is behind the curtain now.

RALPH AS NURSE (O.S.)

" . . . And a good lady, and wise and virtuous.

I nursed her daughter that you talk'd withal . . ."

During RALPH'S lines (which are continuous) WILL stands in the shadow behind the curtain, alone, agitated.

INT. THE ROSE THEATRE. STAGE. DAY.

RALPH AS NURSE

"I tell you, he that can lay hold of her

(he makes the money sign)

Shall have the chinks."

VIOLA AS ROMEO

"Is she a Capulet?
Oh dear account. My life is my foe's debt."

NOL, as "BENVOLIO," at a party, carrying a goblet, tipsy, enters the scene.

NOL AS BENVOLIO

(to ROMEO)

"Away, be gone, the sport is at the best."

VIOLA, about to make her exit, has her hand holding the curtain at the gap.

INT. THE ROSE THEATRE. BEHIND THE CURTAIN. DAY.

WILL is kissing her hand.

INT. THE ROSE THEATRE. STAGE. DAY.

VIOLA AS ROMEO

"Ay, so I fear; the more is my unrest."

INT. THE ROSE THEATRE. BEHIND THE CURTAIN. DAY.

VIOLA comes through the curtain. WILL and VIOLA kiss, dangerously—they are in a narrow space, hidden from the general backstage area.

SAM AS JULIET (O.S.)

"Come hither nurse. What is yond gentleman?"

VIOLA

(to Will)

Oh let it be night!

INT. THE ROSE THEATRE. STAGE. DAY.

RALPH AS NURSE

"I know not."

SAM AS JULIET

"Go ask his name—If he be married,
My grave is like to be my wedding bed."

INT. THE ROSE THEATRE. BEHIND THE CURTAIN. DAY.

"JULIET'S" line hits WILL between the eyes. WILL pulls away.

VIOLA

Oh, do not go . . .

WILL

I must. I must . . .

INT. THE ROSE THEATRE. BACKSTAGE. DAY.

As WILL races up the ladder to his writer's corner, the rehearsal can be heard continuing.

RALPH AS NURSE (O.S.)

"His name is Romeo, and a Montague,
The only son of your great enemy."

ALLEYN (O.S.)
(roaring from the audience)

Terrible!

INT. THE ROSE THEATRE. WRITER'S CORNER. DAY.

WILL arrives at the top of the building in his writer's corner. He spins round once in a circle, rubs his hands together and spits on the floor. His manuscript is all over the table. We take a peak at the lines he has already written.

*INSERT MANUSCRIPT: "But soft, what light through yonder window breaks?
It is the east and Juliet is the sun."*

VIOLA'S VOICE OVER speaks the line.

VIOLA (VO)

"But soft, what light through yonder window breaks?
It is the east and Juliet is the sun!"

INT. DE LESSEPSES' HOUSE. VIOLA'S BEDROOM. EVENING.

VIOLA
(reading)

"Arise fair sun and kill the envious moon
Who is already sick and pale with grief
That thou her maid art far more fair than she . . . "

VIOLA is in bed, reading the lines from the manuscript page. WILL is in bed with her, reading with her.

VIOLA (Cont'd)

Oh, Will!

WILL

Yes, some of it is speakable.

She has to speak through WILL'S kisses, he is nibbling at her neck and shoulders and she has to bat him away with the pages.

VIOLA

(continuing reading)

"It is my lady, O it is my love!
O that she knew she were!"

INT. THE ROSE THEATRE. STAGE. DAY.

VIOLA continues the speech, edge-to-edge, now in rehearsal, with SAM as "JULIET" sighing on the balcony above her.

VIOLA AS ROMEO

"The brightness of her cheek would shame those stars
As daylight doth a lamp. Her eyes in heaven
Would through the airy region stream so bright
That birds would sing and think it were not night.
See how she leans her cheek upon her hand.
O that I were a glove upon that hand,
That I might touch that cheek.

SAM AS JULIET

(above)

"Ay me."

VIOLA AS ROMEO

"She speaks.
Oh speak again bright angel . . . "

We have abandoned real time. The scene continues CROSS CUT between the STAGE and VIOLA'S BED.

INT. DE LESSEPSES' HOUSE. VIOLA'S BEDROOM. EVENING.

WILL
(reading through VIOLA'S kisses)
"Oh Romeo, Romeo, wherefore art thou Romeo?
Deny thy father and refuse thy name."

INT. THE ROSE THEATRE. STAGE. DAY.

SAM AS JULIET
"Or if thou wilt not, be but sworn my love
And I'll no longer be a Capulet."

VIOLA AS ROMEO
(below)
"Shall I hear more or shall I speak at this?"

INT. DE LESSEPSES' HOUSE. VIOLA'S BEDROOM. NIGHT.

WILL and VIOLA in bed.

WILL
"What man art thou that thus bescreen'd in night
So stumblest on my counsel?"

INT. THE ROSE THEATRE. STAGE/AUDITORIUM. NIGHT.

It's become late and the rehearsal is continuing by torchlight.

VIOLA AS ROMEO

" . . . By a name
I know not how to tell thee who I am:
My name, dear saint, is hateful to myself
Because it is an enemy to thee . . . "

We see that a group of the other actors have drifted "out front," drawn by the scene. FENNYMAN is there entranced. Clearly, this stuff is a cut above the normal.

INT. DE LESSEPSES' HOUSE. VIOLA'S BEDROOM. NIGHT.

WILL, undressed, strides around the room, feeding "JULIET'S" lines to VIOLA in bed.

WILL

"The orchard walls are high and hard to climb,
And the place death, considering who thou art,
If any of my kinsmen find thee here.
If they do see thee, they will murder thee."

INT. THE ROSE THEATRE. STAGE. NIGHT.

VIOLA AS ROMEO

"Alack, there lies more peril in thine eye,
Than twenty of their swords! Look thou but sweet,
And I am proof against their enmity."

SAM AS JULIET

I would not for the world.

VIOLA AS ROMEO

I have night's cloak to hide me from their eyes;
And but thou love me, let them find me here.

INT. DE LESSEPSES' HOUSE. VIOLA'S BEDROOM. NIGHT.

WILL and VIOLA are both out of bed, halfway through dressing. Still rehearsing.

WILL

"Good night, good night. As sweet repose and rest
Come to thy heart as that within my breast.
O wilt thou leave me so unsatisfied?"

VIOLA

That's my line!

WILL

Oh, but it is mine too!

INT. THE ROSE THEATRE. STAGE. NIGHT.

VIOLA AS ROMEO

"O wilt thou leave me so unsatisfied?"

SAM AS JULIET

"What satisfaction can'st thou have tonight?"

VIOLA AS ROMEO

"The exchange of thy love's faithful vow for mine."

INT. DE LESSEPSES' HOUSE. VIOLA'S BEDROOM. NIGHT.

WILL and VIOLA are back on the bed, kissing and making love.

WILL

"My bounty is as boundless as the sea,
My love as deep: . . .

VIOLA AND WILL

(continuing the speech with him)

. . . the more I give to thee
The more I have, for both are infinite."

Outside the NURSE is knocking on the door and calling.

INT. THE ROSE THEATRE. STAGE. DAY.

SAM AS JULIET

"I hear some noise within.
Dear love, adieu."

RALPH, the Nurse, calls "JULIET!" off stage.

INT. DE LESSEPSES' HOUSE. VIOLA'S BEDROOM. NIGHT.

VIOLA

(calling to the NURSE who is outside)

Anon, good Nurse—

INT. DE LESSEPSES' HOUSE. OUTSIDE VIOLA'S BEDROOM. NIGHT.

The NURSE listens at the door.

INT. THE ROSE THEATRE. STAGE. DAY.

SAM AS JULIET

"Anon, good Nurse—Sweet Montague be true."

INT. DE LESSEPSES' HOUSE. VIOLA'S BEDROOM. NIGHT.

WILL

"Stay but a little, I will come again."

VIOLA slaps him playfully for his vulgarity, and then kisses him.

INT. THE ROSE THEATRE. STAGE. DAY.

SAM AS JULIET

"Stay but a little, I will come again."

SAM leaves the balcony through the curtain.

VIOLA AS ROMEO

"Oh blessed blessed night."

INT. DE LESSEPSES' HOUSE. VIOLA'S BEDROOM. NIGHT.

It is night. They have just made love. Suddenly it is very still.

VIOLA

(almost to herself)

"I am afeared,
Being in night, all this is but a dream,
Too flattering-sweet to be substantial."

INT. THE ROSE THEATRE. BACKSTAGE. DAY.

Onstage, the scene continues. Backstage NED ALLEYN is working his way upstairs. He passes by RALPH (the Nurse) who has a couple of words "off," as it were, in "JULIET'S" chamber.

SAM AS JULIET (O.S.)

" . . . All my fortunes at thy foot I'll lay,
And follow thee my lord throughout the world."

RALPH AS NURSE

"Madam!"

SAM AS JULIET (O.S.)

"I come, anon—But if thou meanest not well,
I do beseech thee—"

RALPH AS NURSE

"Madam!"

SAM AS JULIET (O.S.)

"By and by I come—
To cease thy strife and leave me to my grief.
A thousand times good night!"

SAM exits (i.e. enters to us) through the curtain

SAM

(to NED)

I cannot move in this dress! and it makes me look like a pig! I have no neck in this pig dress!

(and then hearing his cue from "ROMEO")

Oh, she's off again! She says she's going and then she doesn't.

INT. THE ROSE THEATRE. WRITER'S CORNER. DAY.

NED is arriving. WILL is busy writing. PETER is there, holding the pages WILL has completed, and waiting for WILL to finish his page. PETER is reading his pages. WILL sees NED arrive. He gives his page to PETER.

WILL

(to PETER)

How is it?

PETER

(shrugs)

It's all right.

Typical!, says WILL'S face. Peter departs, leaving the field to NED. WILL braces himself.

WILL

Ned . . . I know . . . I know . . . .

ALLEYN

It's good.

WILL

Oh . . .

ALLEYN

The title won't do.

WILL

Ah . . .

ALLEYN

Romeo and Juliet—just a suggestion.

WILL

Thank you, Ned.

The whole exchange is in ironic code, between old soldiers. NED nods curtly and turns to descend.

WILL (Cont'd)

You are a gentleman.

ALLEYN

And you are a Warwickshire shit-house.

INT. THE ROSE THEATRE. STAGE/AUDITORIUM. DAY.

PETER is just handing the pages to HENSLOWE in the auditorium. HENSLOWE has acquired a performing dog. The dog does somersaults tirelessly. As PETER hands over the pages, he shakes his head.

HENSLOWE

(in disbelief)

You mean, no dog of any kind?

FENNYMAN, the born-again theatre groupie shushes HENSLOWE and looks daggers at him.

PETER

(to HENSLOWE)

The Friar marries them in secret, then Ned gets into a fight with one of the Capulets, Romeo tries to stop them, he gets in Ned's way, I mean in Mercutio's way, so Tybalt kills Mercutio and then Romeo kills Tybalt. Then the Prince banishes him from Verona.

HENSLOWE

(much relieved)

That must be when he goes on the voyage and gets shipwrecked on the island of the Pirate King.

FENNYMAN can't bear it. He storms over. Kicks the dog, roars at HENSLOWE.

FENNYMAN

Cease your prattling! Get out!

(to the stage where the action has paused)

A thousand apologies!

SAM AS JULIET

"Good night, good night. Parting is such sweet sorrow
That I shall say good night till it be morrow."

INT. DE LESSEPSES' HOUSE. VIOLA'S BEDROOM. MORNING.

A sunbeam wakes the lovers. Sunday morning. Church bells. VIOLA wakes with a start. Something is bothering her, she can't think what. WILL calms her.

WILL

Sunday . . . it is Sunday.

He brings her back down to the pillow.

WILL (Cont'd)

I found something in my sleep. The Friar who married them will take up their destinies.

VIOLA

Oh, but it will end well for love?

WILL

In heaven, perhaps. It is not a comedy I am writing now. A broad river divides my lovers—family, duty, fate—as unchangeable as nature.

VIOLA

(sobered)

Yes, this is not life, Will. This is a stolen season.

Suddenly there is a great racket heard from downstairs . . . a man shouting.

WESSEX (O.S.)

Not ready? Where is she?

NURSE (O.S.)

Be patient, my lord, she is dressing.

WESSEX (O.S.)

Will you ask Her Majesty to be patient?!

VIOLA remembers. She jumps up and gives a cry.

VIOLA

Sunday! Greenwich!

INT. DE LESSEPSES' HOUSE. OUTSIDE VIOLA'S BEDROOM. MORNING.

The NURSE is barring the stairs to WESSEX.

WESSEX

Now, pay attention, Nursy. The Queen, Gloriana Regina, God's Chosen Vessel, the Radiant One, who shines her light on us, is at Greenwich today, and prepared, during the evening's festivities, to bestow her gracious favour on my choice of wife—and if we're late for lunch, the old boot will not forgive. So get you to my lady's chamber and produce her with or without her undergarments.

INT. DE LESSEPSES' HOUSE. VIOLA'S BEDROOM. MORNING.

VIOLA has her dress on and is putting on her shoes. WILL, in his underwear is in mid-argument.

WILL

You cannot! Not for the Queen herself!

VIOLA

What will you have me do? Marry you instead?

WILL

(brought up short)

To be the wife of a poor player?—can I wish that for Lady Viola, except in my dreams? And yet I would, if I were free to follow my desire in the harsh light of day.

VIOLA

(tartly)

You follow your desire freely enough in the night. So, if that is all, to Greenwich I go.

WILL

Then I will go with you.

VIOLA

You cannot, Wessex will kill you—

WILL

I know how to fight!

VIOLA

(now fixing her hair)

Stage fighting!

(turning to him)

Oh, Will! As Thomas Kent my heart belongs to you but as Viola the river divides us, and I will marry Wessex a week from Saturday

INT. DE LESSEPSES' HOUSE. OUTSIDE VIOLA'S BEDROOM DOWNSTAIRS HALL. MORNING

The ranting from WESSEX has continued . . .

WESSEX

(ranting)

By heaven, I will drag her down, by the Queen's command . . .

And is cut off short as VIOLA'S door opens at the top of the stairs.

VIOLA

Good morning, my lord!

WESSEX

(impressed by her appearance)

Ah! My lady! The tide waits for no man, but I swear it would wait for you!

VIOLA comes down the stairs. Behind her WILL appears gowned and bonneted. He has also assumed a country accent.

WILL

Here we come at last, my lord!

WESSEX

(taken aback)

Are you bringing your laundry woman?

WILL

Her chaperone. My lady's country cousin.

(arriving with a curtsey)

My, but you be a handsome gallant, just as she said! You may call me Miss Wilhelmina!

WESSEX

On a more fortuitous occasion, perhaps—

WILL

Oh, my lord, you will not shake me off, she never needed me more, I swear by your breeches!

EXT. GREENWICH PALACE NIGHT.

Fireworks explode in the evening sky over Greenwich, a royal palace, crowded now with noble guests.

EXT GREENWICH PALACE. TERRACE. NIGHT.

The way these royal routs work is that the guests mill about, chatting, bowing and generally behaving gallantly, while QUEEN ELIZABETH creates a vortex around her as she passes through the throng, occasionally honouring somebody with a couple of words, until she arrives thankfully at the best chair . . . where she establishes a headquarters. Her current LORD IN WAITING ferries the lucky few forward to a brief audience with the QUEEN, each giving way to the next. VIOLA and WESSEX are, respectively, dipping and bowing as they are greeted by people who know them . . . WILL, in close attendance, joins in gratuitously, bowing until VIOLA nudges him and reminds him to curtsey instead. The QUEEN'S LORD IN WAITING plucks WESSEX'S sleeve.

WESSEX
(to him)

Now?

LORD IN WAITING

Now.

WESSEX
(to Viola)

The Queen asks for you. Answer well.

The LORD IN WAITING ushers VIOLA through the crowd. WILL starts to follow. WESSEX takes him by the arm.

WESSEX (Cont'd)

Is there a man?

WILL

A man, my lord?

WESSEX
(impatiently)

There was a man, a poet—a theatre poet, I heard—does he come to the house?

WILL

A theatre poet?

WESSEX

An insolent penny-a-page rogue, Marlowe, he said, Christopher Marlowe—has he been to the house?

WILL

Marlowe? Oh yes, he is the one, lovely waistcoat, shame about the poetry.

WESSEX
(venomously)

That dog!

ANGLE on the QUEEN.

The LORD IN WAITING has presented VIOLA. VIOLA speaks from a frozen curtsey.

VIOLA

Your Majesty.

QUEEN

Stand up straight, girl.

VIOLA straightens. The QUEEN examines her.

QUEEN (Cont'd)

I have seen you. You are the one who comes to all the plays—at Whitehall, at Richmond.

VIOLA

(agreeing)

Your Majesty.

QUEEN

What do you love so much?

VIOLA

Your Majesty . . .

QUEEN

Speak out! I know who I am. Do you love stories of kings and queens? Feats of arms? Or is it courtly love?

VIOLA

I love theatre. To have stories acted for me by a company of fellows is indeed—

QUEEN

(interrupting)

They are not acted for you, they are acted for me.

VIOLA remains silent, in apology.

ANGLE on WILL.

He is watching and listening. He has never seen the QUEEN so close. He is fascinated.

QUEEN (Cont'd)

And—?

VIOLA

And I love poetry above all.

QUEEN

Above Lord Wessex?

She looks over VIOLA'S shoulder and VIOLA realises WESSEX has moved up behind her. WESSEX bows.

QUEEN (Cont'd)

(to WESSEX)

My lord—when you cannot find your wife you had better look for her at the playhouse.

The COURTIERS titter at her pleasantry.

QUEEN (Cont'd)

But playwrights teach nothing about love, they make it pretty, they make it comical, or they make it lust. They cannot make it true.

VIOLA

(blurts)

Oh, but they can!

She has forgotten herself. The COURTIERS gasp. The QUEEN considers her. WESSEX looks furious. WILL is touched.

VIOLA (Cont'd)

I mean . . . Your Majesty, they do not, they have not, but I believe there is one who can—

WESSEX

Lady Viola is . . . young in the world. Your Majesty is wise in it. Nature and truth are the very enemies of playacting. I'll wager my fortune.

QUEEN

I thought you were here because you had none.

Titters again. WESSEX could kill somebody.

QUEEN (Cont'd)

(by way of dismissing him)

Well, no one will take your wager, it seems.

WILL

Fifty pounds!

Shock and horror. QUEEN ELIZABETH is the only person amused.

QUEEN

Fifty pounds! A very worthy sum on a very worthy question. Can a play show us the very truth and nature of love? I bear witness to the wager, and will be the judge of it as occasion arises.

(which wins a scatter of applause. She gathers her skirts and stands)

I have not seen anything to settle it yet.

(she moves away, everybody bowing and scraping)

So—the fireworks will be soothing after the excitements of Lady Viola's audience.

(and now she is next to WESSEX who is bowing low. Intimately to him)

Have her then, but you are a lordly fool. She has been plucked since I saw her last, and not by you. It takes a woman to know it.

The QUEEN passes by, and as WESSEX comes vertical again, we see his face a mask of furious realisation.

WESSEX
(to himself)
Marlowe!

INT. BURBAGE'S HOUSE. ENTRANCE. DAY.

CHRISTOPHER MARLOWE shuts the door behind him. Above him, the ceiling creaks to the rhythm of copulation. He has a sheaf of manuscript pages in his hand. He goes to the stairs.

MARLOWE
Burbage!

The creaking stops.

BURBAGE'S VOICE
Who's there?

INT. BURBAGE'S HOUSE. STAIRS. DAY.

MARLOWE ascends.

MARLOWE
Marlowe.

BURBAGE'S VOICE
Kit!

INT. BURBAGE'S HOUSE. BEDROOM. DAY.

MARLOWE enters, ignoring the situation on the bed where ROSALINE is astride BURBAGE.

MARLOWE

You are playing my *Faustus* this afternoon. Don't spend yourself in sport.

ROSALINE

(working hard)

This afternoon!—we'll still be here this afternoon.

BURBAGE

What do you want, Kit?

MARLOWE

My *Massacre at Paris* is complete.

BURBAGE

You have the last act?

MARLOWE

You have the money?

BURBAGE

Tomorrow.

MARLOWE

(leaving)

Then tomorrow you will have the pages.

BURBAGE

Wait!

(to ROSALINE)

Will you desist!

MARLOWE

Twenty pounds on delivery.

BURBAGE

What is money to men like us? Besides, if I need a play, I have another waiting, a comedy by Shakespeare.

MARLOWE

Romeo?—he gave it to Henslowe.

BURBAGE

Never!

MARLOWE

Well, I am to Deptford now, I leave my respects, Miss Rosaline.

BURBAGE

I gave Shakespeare two sovereigns for *Romeo*!

MARLOWE

(leaving)

You did. But Ned Alleyn and the Admiral's Men have the playing of it at the Rose.

BURBAGE

Treachery!

BURBAGE rouses himself violently, throwing ROSALINE off the bed. The glass bracelet is flung from her wrist. It breaks on the floor, releasing a strip of paper. BURBAGE picks it up. What he reads on it does not please him: it is WILL'S signature.

BURBAGE (Cont'd)

Traitor and thief!

EXT. STREETS. DAY.

BURBAGE and a solid wedge of the CHAMBERLAIN'S MEN are cleaving a path through the crowds. Their faces are grim.

INT. THE ROSE THEATRE. STAGE/AUDITORIUM/UNDER THE STAGE. DAY.

We are in Act III Scene I. NED ALLEYN as "MERCUTIO" and NOL as "BENVOLIO", and two "MONTAGUE" sidekicks are in occupation of the stage, when the "CAPULETS" swagger in, four of them headed by JAMES HEMMINGS as "TYBALT."

NOL AS BENVOLIO

"By my head, here comes the Capulets."

ALLEYN AS MERCUTIO

"By my heel, I care not."

JAMES HEMMINGS AS TYBALT

"Follow me close, for I will speak to them.
(with bombast to "MERCUTIO")
Gentlemen, good e'en: a word with one of you."

NED comes out of character.

ALLEYN

Are you going to do it like that? And before the humbled actor can reply NED continues.

ALLEYN (As MERCUTIO)

And but one word with one of us? Couple it with something, make it a word and a blow.

But suddenly six more men and a dog invade the stage, ready to fight.

BURBAGE and the CHAMBERLAIN'S MEN have arrived to avenge BURBAGE'S honour with swords, clubs, and a bucket (containing pig swill).

BURBAGE

Where is that thieving hack who can't keep his pen in his own ink pot!?

WILL has already leapt up onto the stage.

WILL

What is this rabble?!

BURBAGE aims a blow at WILL, who ducks and grabs a stave from the nearest actor, and parries the blow. He swings at BURBAGE, a CHAMBERLAIN'S MAN swings at WILL, THOMAS cries out, someone else slashes the stage hangings bringing down the drapes, and in a moment the ADMIRAL'S MEN and the CHAMBERLAIN'S MEN, using their much rehearsed skills, are brawling with weapons and fists, using everything short of unbuttoned rapiers. CRAB, the dog, is yapping and snapping at any legs he can reach. HENSLOWE, a little slow to catch up on the situation, checks the page in his hand. FENNYMAN, much slower to catch up, watches enthralled.

FENNYMAN
(*to HENSLOWE*)

Wonderful, wonderful! And a dog!

But now HENSLOWE has worked out that these actors don't belong, nor does the scene. He enters the fray, but his interest is protecting his property. Big burly RALPH is using a couple of unlit torches as weapons; he breaks one of them over an enemy's back and HENSLOWE turns on RALPH.

HENSLOWE

Not with my props!

VIOLA is doing well enough, tripping up an enemy with a well-judged stave, and then using it to deflect a blow aimed at WILL.

VIOLA

Will! What—?

WILL

A literary feud. Quite normal.

Then he is smashed over the head. He falls off the stage taking VIOLA with him. Under the stage is a space (known as Hell) and WILL shoves VIOLA into this space.

WILL (Cont'd)

Stay hid!

He gets back onto the stage, where the goings on are worthy of the Four Musketeers and Robin Hood combined, with SAM GOSSE, dressed as "JULIET," fighting with the best of them. There is a stack of cushions, stored for the expensive seats, and as the stack is knocked over, NED ALLEYN and others grab cushions to use as shields. Soon cushions are being ripped, and the air is full of flying feathers. The trap door in the stage opens, VIOLA'S head pops up. She looks around and, surrounded by milling legs and floating feathers, a boot catches her sideways and half knocks her wig off. In danger of having her cover blown, she ducks down again, leaving the trap open just nicely for Will to plummet down it.

INT. THE ROSE THEATRE. UNDER THE STAGE. DAY.

WILL

I dreamed last night of a shipwreck. You were cast ashore in a far country.

They embrace and kiss. In a moment they are in a world of their own.

INT. THE ROSE THEATRE. UNDER THE STAGE. DAY.

The battle rages.

FENNYMAN, alone now in the auditorium, continues to watch entranced. It's the greatest show he's ever seen. HENSLOWE is desperately trying to rescue odd props that have been seconded to the fight. Someone picks up a tree that is to be used in Romeo. HENSLOWE yells.

HENSLOWE

We need that for the balcony scene!

FENNYMAN notices this, and it rings a distant bell. He looks around and realises that some of these faces are unfamiliar. The tree comes crashing down on RALPH'S head. FENNYMAN looks at HENSLOWE.

HENSLOWE (Cont'd)
(in despair)

My poor Rose!

He collapses on to a broken bench. FENNYMAN comes over to him, grabs the script pages from his pocket, and consults them to confirm what he has now begun to suspect: that this scene is not in them.

FENNYMAN
(horrified)

My investment! LAMBERT!!!

LAMBERT has been sleeping peacefully through this, but wakes to his master's call.

FENNYMAN (Cont'd)
(points at the fray)

VENGEANCE!

HENSLOWE attempts to intervene.

HENSLOWE

I want no more trouble, Mr. Fennyman. As I explained to you, the theatre business . . .

FENNYMAN

Henslowe, you pound of tripe, in my business I would be out of business if I had your courage, so don't tell me about business . . .

And he delivers a telling blow to a passing CHAMBERLAIN'S MAN, who wheels off the stage. LAMBERT meanwhile is making short work of the rest of the opposition, receiving help with the thorny business of identification from SAM. Stray members of the CHAMBERLAIN'S MEN are running from the theatre, as BURBAGE, fighting a heroic last stand, is tipped backwards by FENNYMAN off the stage and into a bucket of swill.

A PAUSE.

Then NED starts applauding. The others, weary from fighting, start applauding too, from all levels of the theatre. FENNYMAN looks around, starting to beam, as a din of encores and bravos engulf him. A star!

INT. BROTHEL. NIGHT.

The victorious army of actors bursts into the brothel, FENNYMAN at their head. He owns the brothel. The place is already crowded with WHORES and CUSTOMERS. It's a party.

FENNYMAN

(shouts)

A famous victory! Kegs and legs. Open and on the house! Oh what happy hour!

(and grabbing a RADDLED WHORE)

Poxy Pol! You keep yourself to yourself I'll not have you infecting my investment!

VIOLA AS THOMAS

(looking around guardedly. To WILL)

Is this a tavern?

WILL

It is also a tavern.

WILL sits her down in THE COMPANY and takes the chair next to her. A PRETTY WHORE immediately sits on WILL'S knee and kisses him.

PRETTY WHORE

I remember you! The poet!

VIOLA furiously pulls the PRETTY WHORE off WILL'S lap.

PRETTY WHORE (Cont'd)

One at a time, one at a time!

SECOND WHORE

(to VIOLA)

Oh, he's a pretty one! Tell me your story while I tickle your fancy!

VIOLA AS THOMAS

Oh!—it's—it's—oh, it's a house of ill-repute!

WILL

It is, Thomas, but of good reputation. Come, there is no harm in a drink.

Glasses are shoved into their hands. Everyone has a glass. Except RALPH.

RALPH

(declining the glass)

Never when I'm working!

The PRETTY WHORE has turned her attention to SAM. SAM looks uncomfortable.

PRETTY WHORE

Never tried it? Never?

(groping him)

I think you are ready, Sam!

FENNYMAN shouts a toast.

FENNYMAN

(raising his glass)

You are welcome to my best house! Here's to the Admiral's Men!

Everybody drinks. VIOLA drinks too. She decides to enjoy it. She bangs down her glass.

VIOLA AS THOMAS

(shouts)

The Admiral's Men!

WILL toasts with her. He sees that she feels one of THE COMPANY.

EXT. STREET. NIGHT.

A figure is running desperately through the streets. He comes into the square and runs towards the Rose.

INT. BROTHEL. NIGHT.

Half THE COMPANY are singing. NOL and a WHORE are tumbling down the stairs together. He is without his trousers. An awful lot of drink has gone down.

SAM

(to the PRETTIEST WHORE)

I . . . quite liked it.

VIOLA, bright eyed, is banging her glass on the table in time to a song which is being drunkenly delivered by a barbershop quartet of actors.

FENNYMAN reels into VIOLA.

FENNYMAN

Master Kent! You have not dipped your wick?

VIOLA AS THOMAS

(baffled)

My wick?

WILL

(saving her)

Mr. Fennyman, because you love the theatre you must have a part in my play. I am writing an Apothecary, a small but vital role.

FENNYMAN

(embracing WILL)

By heaven, I thank you! I will be your Apothecary!

In his general enthusiasm, he embraces the next man, who is RALPH, stone cold sober.

FENNYMAN (Cont'd)

I am to be in your play.

WHORE

(to RALPH)

And what is this play about?

RALPH

Well, there's this Nurse . . .

FENNYMAN, beside himself, shouts for silence, announcing—

FENNYMAN

Mr. Shakespeare has given me the part of the Apothecary!

HENSLOWE

The Apothecary? Will, what is the story? Where is the shipwreck? How does the comedy end?

WILL

By God, I wish I knew.

HENSLOWE

By God, Will, if you do not, who does? Let us have pirates, clowns, and a happy ending, or we will send you back to Stratford to your wife!

That goes down very well with the entire COMPANY . . . except for VIOLA and WILL. He looks at her, helplessly, then makes as if to say something. VIOLA ducks away from him and blunders blindly out of the street door, in tears.

VIOLA passes PETER who is coming in from the street. WILL, attempting to follow VIOLA, is grabbed round the shoulders by PETER . . . who, we now see, is in a highly emotional state. WILL tries to fight him off but PETER has the strength of the news he brings.

PETER

(shouts)

Will! Mr. Henslowe! Gentlemen all!

He brings the room to silence.

PETER (Cont'd)

A black day for us all! There is news come up river from Deptford. Marlowe is dead.

There are general gasps and cries for information.

PETER (Cont'd)

Stabbed! Stabbed to death in a tavern at Deptford!

No one is more affected than WILL. This second blow is worse than the first. He stands horror-stricken.

WILL

Oh . . . what have I done?

ALLEYN

(standing up)

He was the first man among us. A great light has gone out.

EXT. BROTHEL. NIGHT.

WILL comes staggering out into the street.

WILL

It was I who killed him! God forgive me, God forgive me!

He falls into a stagnant puddle, a deep gutter of water and garbage. He gets up and staggers on.

EXT. CHURCH TOWER. NIGHT.

A church tower looms up in the night sky.

INT. CHURCH. NIGHT.

This is where WILL has come. The church is empty, but for the demented, grieving figure of SHAKESPEARE, kneeling, praying, weeping, banging his head, in his private purgatory, dimly lit by tallow candles, gazed upon by effigies of the dead and images of his Redeemer. He is wet, bedraggled, weeds and leaves in his hair.

EXT. DE LESSEPSES' HOUSE. DAY.

A lovely sunny morning. The church bells are ringing. VIOLA and the NURSE, mounted, approach. VIOLA rides sidesaddle on a beautiful horse, and is followed, rather like Quixote by Sancho, by the NURSE on a less impressive animal.

Riding in the opposite direction, is WESSEX. And what a happy day it is. He sings and hums to himself merrily. Here is a man who has heard wonderful news. He sees VIOLA and greets her merrily.

WESSEX

You look sad, my lady! Let me take you riding.

VIOLA

It is not my riding day, my lord.

WESSEX

Bless me, I thought it was a horse.

VIOLA

I am going to church.

WESSEX

(recomposing his features to solemnity)

I understand of course. It is to be expected.

VIOLA

It is to be expected on a Sunday.

WESSEX

And on a day of mourning. I never met the fellow but once at your house.

VIOLA

(cannot take this in)

Mourning? Who is dead, my lord?

WESSEX

Oh!—dear God, I did not think it would be me to tell you. A great loss to playwriting, and to dancing.

VIOLA almost faints. The NURSE steadies her.

VIOLA

(faintly)

He is dead?

WESSEX

(cheerfully solemn)

Killed last night, in a tavern! Come, then, we'll say a prayer for his soul—

VIOLA gives a silent cry. The NURSE is speaking to her in distress.

NURSE

My lady . . . my lady . . . now is the time to show your breeding.

INT. CHURCH. DAY.

The NURSE is holding VIOLA up as they enter the church. VIOLA seems catatonic. The NURSE lowers her onto a seat and sits down next to her.

As they sit, the CHOIR enters singing. WESSEX, who is sitting in the next pew, looks about him with interest. He hasn't been in a church for years. What he sees turns him to jelly. He sees WILL SHAKESPEARE.

ANGLE on WILL.

WILL is a spectral, bedraggled figure, backlit by a great shaft of light; he would look like a ghost at the best of times, and this is the worst. Bleeding from where he has banged his head, bedraggled and ravaged by the night, he stands in a side chapel staring at WESSEX.

WESSEX gasps and sweats, and sees WILL raise a quivering accusatory finger at him. WESSEX cracks. He starts to mumble.

WESSEX

Oh, spare me, dear ghost, spare me for the love of Christ!

Now VIOLA sees WILL. She is still paralysed, and seems at first unable to take him in. She watches with detachment as WESSEX starts to back out of the church, finally running in terror.

WESSEX (Cont'd)

(screaming)

Spare me!

The CHOIR continues to sing, but the scream brings VIOLA to her senses and she runs to a side door where WILL is leaving.

EXT. CHURCH. DAY.

Outside, VIOLA sees WILL, staggering away from the church. She calls his name.

VIOLA

Will!

He does not answer. She runs after him.

VIOLA (Cont'd)

Oh, my love, I thought you were dead!

She clasps him to her. They hold each other for a moment then WILL pulls back.

WILL

It is worse. I have killed a man.

EXT. MEADOW. DAY.

VIOLA'S horse grazes. WILL lies on his back, still sobered and full of guilt. VIOLA sits on the grass among the buttercups and looks down at him. VIOLA is plaiting a finger-ring from stems of grass. She has not yet revealed her feelings.

WILL

Marlowe's touch was in my *Titus Andronicus* and my *Henry VI* was a house built on his foundations.

VIOLA

You never spoke so well of him.

WILL

He was not dead before. I would exchange all my plays to come for all of his that will never come.

VIOLA

You lie.

WILL turns to look at her.

VIOLA (Cont'd)

You lie in your meadow as you lied in my bed.

WILL

My love is no lie. I have a wife, yes, and I cannot marry the daughter of Sir Robert de Lesseps. It needed no wife come from Stratford to tell you that. And yet you let me come to your bed.

VIOLA

Calf love. I loved the writer, and gave up the prize for a sonnet.

WILL

I was the more deceived.

VIOLA

Yes—you were deceived. For I never loved you till now.

WILL

. . . Now?

VIOLA

(declaring herself)

I love you, Will, beyond poetry.

WILL

Oh, my love . . .

(he kisses her)

You ran from me before.

VIOLA

You were not dead before. When I thought you dead, I did not care about all the plays that will never come, only that I would never see your face. I saw our end, and it will come.

WILL

You cannot marry Wessex!

VIOLA

If not Wessex the Queen will know the cause and there will be no more Will Shakespeare.

They kiss again, passionately.

WILL

No . . . no

VIOLA

(through his kisses)

But I will go to Wessex as a widow from these vows, as solemn as they are unsanctified.

And as their desperate kisses turn into lovemaking we cut to:

INT. THE ROSE THEATRE. STAGE/AUDITORIUM. DAY.

WILL

(he is in mid speech)

. . . For killing Juliet's kinsman Tybalt, the one who killed Romeo's friend Mercutio, Romeo is banished . . .

He is on the stage of the Rose. The entire COMPANY is assembled, HENSLOWE and FENNYMAN included, holding pages of manuscript, which they are sharing together, examining the separated pages, passing pages to each other, etc. WILL'S mood is intense and focussed.

WILL (Cont'd)

. . . but the Friar who married Romeo and Juliet—

ACTOR (EDWARD)

Is that me. Will?

WILL

You, Edward. The Friar who married them gives Juliet a potion to drink. It is a secret potion. It makes her seeming dead. She is placed in the tomb of the Capulets. She will awake to life and love when Romeo comes to her side again.

THE COMPANY murmurs approval.

WILL (Cont'd)

I have not said all. By malign fate, the message goes astray which would tell Romeo of the Friar's plan. He hears only that Juliet is dead. And thus he goes to the Apothecary.

FENNYMAN

That's me.

WILL

And buys a deadly poison. He enters the tomb to say farewell to Juliet who lies there cold as death. He drinks the poison. He dies by her side. And then she wakes and sees him dead.

HENSLOWE is fascinated and appalled.

WILL (Cont'd)

And so Juliet takes his dagger and kills herself.

PAUSE.

WILL is staring at VIOLA.

HENSLOWE

Well, that will have them rolling in the aisles.

FENNYMAN

Sad and wonderful! I have a blue velvet cap which will do well, I have seen an apothecary with a cap just so.

ALLEYN

(to WILL)

Yes—it will serve. But there's a scene missing between marriage and death.

WILL is still staring at VIOLA. Aware, suddenly, of the others watching, she breaks his gaze and drops her head.

WILL looks at NED.

INT. DE LESSEPSES' HOUSE. VIOLA'S BEDROOM. EVENING.

WILL and VIOLA. VIOLA dressed as THOMAS. He has a present for her—a neatly written manuscript of his play, on sheets folded to octavo size.

WILL

The play. All written out for you. I had the clerk at Bridewell do it, he has a good fist for lettering.

She wants to accept the present with joy, but something in his mood restrains her.

WILL (Cont'd)

There's a new scene . . .

He turns the pages and shows her.

VIOLA

Will you read it for me?

WILL

(he knows it)

"Wilt thou be gone? It is not yet near day.
It was the nightingale and not the lark
That pierced the fearful hollow of thine ear.
Nightly she sings on yon pomegranate tree.
Believe me, love, it was the nightingale."

VIOLA

(reading)

"It was the lark, the herald of the morn,
No nightingale. Look, love, what envious streaks
Do lace the severing clouds in yonder east.
Night's candles are burnt out, and jocund day
Stands tiptoe on the misty mountain tops.
I must be gone and live, or stay and die."

The words of the scene become WILL'S and VIOLA'S, their way of saying the farewells they cannot utter.

WILL

"Yon light is not daylight, I know it, I.
It is some meteor that the sun exhales
To be to thee this night a torchbearer . . . "

INT. THE ROSE THEATRE. BACKSTAGE. DAY.

But the scene is continuing with VIOLA dressed as "THOMAS."

Somewhere behind and up above the stage, in a deserted corner among rigging, bits of scenery, etc., they speak the lines and we hardly know ourselves whether it is rehearsal or lovemaking. But after a few moments it is definitely lovemaking. Their clothes start coming away, their words interrupted by kisses.

WILL

" . . . thou need'st not to be gone."

VIOLA

"I have more care to stay than will to go.
Come death, and welcome. Juliet wills it so.
How is't my soul? Let's talk. It is not day."

By now, her loosened bosom-bandage has been pulled away and WILL passionately embraces her nakedness.

And into this heaving composition comes a little white mouse, unseen by them, climbing through a knot hole in the planking behind VIOLA'S head.

An adjacent knot hole reveals a human eye and we do not need to be told it is JOHN WEBSTER'S.

WEBSTER takes his eye away from the peephole, and frowns, thinking it out.

EXT. ALLEWAY. DAY.

TILNEY puts a coin in WEBSTER'S hand.

TILNEY

You will go far, I fear.

TILNEY (Cont'd)

I hope we work together again.

Tilney walks away.

EXT. THE ROSE THEATRE. DAY.

A man is pacing up and down, in a sort of agony. He is muttering. He is glancing at a sheet of paper. He is FENNYMAN rehearsing the important role of the Apothecary, for which he has a special voice.

FENNYMAN

"Such mortal drugs I have but Mantua's law
Is death to any he that utters them."
Then him. Then me.
"Put this in any liquid thing you will
And . . . "—something—

He has dried up. He curses—the terror and despair.

FENNYMAN (Cont'd)

"Such mortal drugs I have . . . "
What is it? What is it?

He is so wrapped up in all this that he simply does not notice when WESSEX rides up to the main entrance dismounts and walks inside.

INT. THE ROSE THEATRE. STAGE/AUDITORIUM. DAY.

Onstage, the rehearsal continues. WESSEX strides in. Among the audience are HENSLOWE, a few actors . . .and JOHN WEBSTER . . . who sees WESSEX and jumps up and goes to him.

WEBSTER

My lord!

WESSEX knocks him aside and continues.

WESSEX
(shouts)

Shakespeare!

Everything stops.

WESSEX (Cont'd)

You upstart inky pup! Now I will show you your place, which is in hell!

WILL

You are on my ground.

WESSEX

(drawing his sword)

By God, I'll fight the lot of you—

WILL draws his sword.

WILL

I am more than enough.

VIOLA reacts. She almost gives herself away. But the fight has started.

WESSEX slashes at WILL. WILL knows how to fight. He parries and thrusts. WESSEX is surprised. The fight goes fast and furious around the stage, until WILL thrusts accurately at WESSEX'S chest . . . and would have killed him but for the button on his sword-point.

WESSEX grapples with him, and now it becomes a parody of the Hamlet duel; WESSEX'S unbuttoned sword falls to the ground, WILL puts his foot on it, tosses WESSEX his own safe sword, picks up Wessex's sword and continues the fight until he has WESSEX at his mercy.

WILL has fought with a passionate rage that has everybody staring at him. Now the look in his eyes is merciless.

WILL (Cont'd)

Absent friends!

(to the assembly)

This is the murderer of Kit Marlowe!

NED ALLEYN comes forward looking worried and dubious.

ALLEYN

Will . . .

WESSEX

I rejoiced at his death because I thought it was yours. That is all I know of Marlowe.

ALLEYN

It's true, Will—it was a tavern brawl . . . Marlowe attacked, and got his own knife in the eye. A quarrel about the bill . . .

HENSLOWE

The bill! Oh, vanity, vanity!

ALLEYN

Not the billing, the bill!

WILL steps back, and sinks to his knees. His relief could not be greater.

WILL

(to the heavens)

Oh God, I am free of it!

WESSEX gets to his feet. TILNEY enters the auditorium from the public entrance.

WESSEX

Close it!

TILNEY

My Lord Wessex!

WESSEX

(foaming)

Close it! Take it down stone by stone! I want it ploughed into the ground, and sown with quick lime!

WESSEX storms out past the bewildered TILNEY.

HENSLOWE

Mr. Tilney, what is this?

TILNEY

Sedition and indecency!

HENSLOWE

What?!

WEBSTER

Master of the Revels, sir, over here, sir.

TILNEY

(to WEBSTER)

Where, boy?

WEBSTER

(points)

I saw her bubbies!

TILNEY

(shocked and gratified)

A woman on the stage? A woman?

WEBSTER

I swear it!

THE COMPANY of actors are dumbstruck. None more than VIOLA.

TILNEY

So, Henslowe! I say this theatre is closed! On the authority of the powers invested in me by the court—I close this theatre!

HENSLOWE

Why so?

TILNEY

(triumphantly)

For lewdness and unshamefacedness! For displaying a female on the public stage!

TILNEY is unstoppable. He jumps on the stage . . . and seizes SAM GOSSE. Before WEBSTER or anyone can intervene, TILNEY pulls up his skirt,ignoring SAM'S rather gutteral yells of protest and pulls down SAM'S drawers.

TILNEY's face is a study. So is everybody else's. WEBSTER rolls his eyes (oh, these stupid grown-ups!) and deftly throws one of his mice onto "ROMEO'S" hair. VIOLA gives a shrill scream, the startled mouse descends her neck via VIOLA'S ear, and seeks an entry into her collar. By which time VIOLA has gone berserk and torn off her wig. Her hair is pinned up but there is no question about her gender.

WILL is paralysed. VIOLA gives him a look of terrible despair and apology.

WEBSTER
(pointing at SAM)

Not him.

(pointing at VIOLA)

—her.

HENSLOWE

He's a woman!

By now the scene is playing to a crowded theatre, or so it seems.

TILNEY

That's who I meant! This theatre is closed! Notice will be posted!

SAM has picked himself up, and his drawers.

HENSLOWE
(to NED)

Ned, I swear I knew nothing of this!

VIOLA
(hoping to protect WILL)

Nobody knew!

WEBSTER

(pointing at WILL)

He did! I saw him kissing her bubbies!

Everybody looks at WILL, who stares at VIOLA, helpless.

TILNEY

Closed! Closed, mark you, Henslowe!

TILNEY turns on his heel and leaves in triumph. THE COMPANY is still polaxed.

HENSLOWE

(in despair)

It is over.

VIOLA

I am so sorry, Mr. Henslowe. I wanted to be an actor .

(she turns to WILL)

I am sorry, Will.

WILL shakes his head. This cannot be the end.

VIOLA walks away, leaving by the public entrance. They all let her go, watching her silently. As she passes WABASH . . .

WABASH

Y-y-y-you w-w-w-were w-w-w-w-wonderful.

VIOLA

Thank you.

As she is leaving, WILL comes to life. He starts off towards her . . . but his progress is halted by a sock to the jaw from NED ALLEYN. WILL falls down in the dust.

FENNYMAN enters, still bent over his sheet of paper, mumbling his precious lines. When he reaches the groundlings yard, he finds to his surprise the whole COMPANY is standing about in attitudes of despair or worse. FENNYMAN looks around.

FENNYMAN

Everything all right?

EXT. THE ROSE THEATRE. EVENING.

The closure notice is nailed to the door.

INT. DE LESSEPSES' HOUSE. VIOLA'S BEDROOM. NIGHT.

VIOLA, in her nightdress, is reading by candlelight. She is reading her private manuscript of Romeo and Juliet *. . . and rereading. Next to her is a tray of covered dishes. The NURSE enters and looks at her sympathetically. She lifts the tray. She realises it is heavy. She puts it down and raises the covers and sees that VIOLA has eaten nothing.*

She looks at VIOLA'S tears, but there is nothing to be said.

INT. TAVERN. DAY.

They are all there—the ADMIRAL'S MEN, including WILL and HENSLOWE, drowning their sorrows. Everyone is drunk. FENNYMAN is also there, taking the disaster somewhat selfishly.

FENNYMAN

(muttering)

I would have been good . . . I would have been great.

He hands a flask to RALPH who is in a similar mood.

RALPH

So would I. We both would.

RALPH contemplates the flask, and, since he's not working, takes a swig. A moment later, he keels over, rigid as a pole.

The street door crashes open. BURBAGE enters. Behind him enter a solid wedge of the CHAMBERLAIN'S MEN, sober-faced, several with black eyes and bandages round their heads.

FENNYMAN
(shouts)

Lambert!

LAMBERT, FENNYMAN'S henchman and killer, puts down his tankard and comes forward, casually kicking chairs and tables out of his way.

FENNYMAN (Cont'd)

Kill him!

LAMBERT reaches up to the wall over the bar and takes down once of the ceremonial weapons hanging there—a battle-axe.

But BURBAGE has a flintlock pistol stuck into his sash. BURBAGE draws and the pistol roars, shooting flame, LAMBERT curses, drops the axe, nurses his wounded hand. BURBAGE puts the pistol back into his sash. NED ALLEYN is half-drunk at a table. He staggers to his feet. He faces BURBAGE.

ALLEYN

Well, Burbage—you never did know when your scene was over.

BURBAGE

That can wait. The Master of the Revels despises us for vagrants, tinkers, and peddlers of bombast. But my father, James Burbage, had the first licence to make a company of players from Her Majesty, and he drew from poets the literature of the age. Their fame will be our fame. So let them all know, we are men of parts. We are a brotherhood, and we will be a profession. Will Shakespeare has a play. I have a theatre. The Curtain is yours.

EXT. THE CURTAIN THEATRE. DAY.

A strong wind is blowing through the trees. A BOY with a paste-pot and a bundle of flyers, is having trouble pasting a flyer on the wall of the building. A gust of wind scatters the bundle and sends a couple of dozen flyers flying into the sky. The BOY with the paste-pot runs around, trying to recover those he can. We look at the poster. It says

By permission of
MR. BURBAGE
A
HUGH FENNYMAN PRODUCTION
OF
MR. HENSLOWE'S PRESENTATION
OF
THE ADMIRAL'S MEN IN PERFORMANCE
OF
THE EXCELLENT AND LAMENTABLE TRAGEDY
OF
ROMEO AND JULIET
with Mr. Fennyman as the Apothecary

WILL comes out of the theatre, and passes the poster. He walks on without looking at it. A voice calls after him:

HENSLOWE

Will!

WILL does not turn to look at him.

HENSLOWE (Cont'd)

We'll be needing a Romeo . . .

WILL carries on walking.

EXT. STREETS. DAY.

WILL is pushing through the crowds on his way to the river.

INT. DE LESSEPSES' HOUSE. VIOLA'S BEDROOM. DAY.

The NURSE is helping VIOLA to dress—in a wedding dress. The NURSE is in tears. VIOLA submits to the task impassively.

EXT. THE RIVER. DAY.

WILL is climbing down the ladder to the waiting boats.

INT. DE LESSEPSES' HOUSE. HALL. DAY.

WESSEX, dressed to be a bridegroom, is concluding his negotiations with DE LESSEPS, while LADY DE LESSEPS weeps. DE LESSEPS is signing papers. There is a money chest, too.

WESSEX

My ship is moored at Bankside, bound for Virginia on the afternoon tide—please do not weep, Lady De Lesseps, you are gaining a colony.

DE LESSEPS

And you are gaining five thousand pounds, my lord . . . by these drafts in my hand.

WESSEX

Would you oblige me with fifty or so in gold?—just to settle my accounts at the dockside?

DE LESSEPS sighs and unlocks his money chest. WESSEX places his empty purse on the desk.

WESSEX (Cont'd)

Ah!—Look, she comes!

VIOLA has appeared at the top of the stairs with the NURSE.

VIOLA

Good morning, my lord. I see you are open for business—so let's to church.

EXT. DE LESSEPSES' HOUSE. DAY.

WILL is running across the grass towards the house. As he crosses the bridge over the moat, a carriage bears down on him, and he has to flatten himself against the wall of the gatehouse as the carriage passes, taking WESSEX and his bride to church.

WILL'S face, as he watches the carriage disappear. Distant bells begin to peal.

EXT. CHURCH DOOR. DAY.

The bells announce the completion of the marriage—as WESSEX and the new LADY WESSEX leave the church. VIOLA'S veil is flying in the wind, and beneath it we can just see VIOLA'S unhappy face. The DE LESSEPS FAMILY entourage is applauding. WESSEX beams with satisfaction.

Suddenly the sky and the wind deliver a message—a flyer from the Curtain slaps against WESSEX'S face. He claws at it and tries to throw it away. The wind delivers it to VIOLA'S bosom. She takes it up and reads it. And passes it to the NURSE.

WESSEX descends the steps to where the curtained carriage awaits the bride and groom. He gallantly holds the door for VIOLA to enter. She climbs aboard. WESSEX makes to follow her.

NURSE

My lord!

The NURSE grasps him in a moving embrace, to WESSEX'S discomfort.

NURSE (Cont'd)

Be good to her, my lord!

WESSEX

I will.

He tries to disengage. She won't have it.

NURSE

God bless you!

WESSEX

Thank you. Let go, there's a good nurse.

After a couple of further attempts, WESSEX extricates himself.

WESSEX (Cont'd)

The tide will not wait. Farewell!

WESSEX approaches the carriage.

WESSEX (Cont'd)

You will all be welcome in Virginia.

WESSEX pulls aside the curtain and gets in.

INT. CARRIAGE. DAY.

It takes a moment for WESSEX to realise he is alone in there. He looks around but VIOLA has fled.

EXT. THE CURTAIN THEATRE. DAY.

Hundreds of people are converging on the theatre. Among them is the Puritan MAKEPEACE, vainly exhorting the crowds to run away from sin . . .

MAKEPEACE

Licentiousness is made a show, vice is made a show, vanity and pride likewise made a show! This is the very business of show . . .

But MAKEPEACE is being carried inexorably through the main doors of the theatre.

INT. THE CURTAIN THEATRE. BACKSTAGE. DAY.

The ADMIRAL'S MEN are all in costume, and are in a buzz of nervous excitement. ALLEYN, dressed for "MERCUTIO," is giving last minute instructions to PETER. JAMES and JOHN HEMMINGS are arguing about the timing of their entrance. FENNYMAN in his apothecary's cap is agonising over his lines. WABASH is stuttering over his. Alone in his dejection in the midst of all this, is WILL, dressed for "ROMEO."

FENNYMAN approaches him, apothecary's cap in hand.

FENNYMAN

Is this all right?

WILL nods, miserable.

SAM has found a private corner. He is gargling into a basin. He looks worried and furtive.

INT. THE CURTAIN THEATRE. AUDITORIUM. DAY.

The audience is gathering.

EXT. THE CURTAIN THEATRE. DAY.

Word has got around. Even rich people are coming. They arrive by carriage and by palanquin. Some of them are cloaked and hooded, slumming incognito. A cannon booms from the Curtain. The flag of the ADMIRAL'S MEN flutters above.

EXT. THE CURTAIN THEATRE. ENTRANCE. DAY.

LAMBERT and FREES are taking the entrance money.

INT. THE CURTAIN THEATRE. AUDITORIUM. DAY.

The auditorium is now packed. Among them, sheepish, is MAKEPEACE.

INT. THE CURTAIN THEATRE. BACKSTAGE. DAY.

Everything is ready. NED signals the musicians. Trumpets and drums sound. The house falls silent.

INT. THE CURTAIN THEATRE. THE WINGS. DAY.

WABASH seems to be important at the beginning. We have never been told what part he plays. He is still muttering lines and stuttering them.

WABASH
(mutter)
T-t-t-two h-h-households b-both alike in d-d-d-dignity.

WILL listens to him in agony. He finds HENSLOWE next to him.

WILL
(to HENSLOWE)
We are lost.

HENSLOWE

No, it will turn out well.

WILL

How will it?

HENSLOWE

I don't know, it's a mystery.

And off we go. HENSLOWE claps WABASH on the shoulder and sends him through the curtain.

ANGLE on WABASH.

INT. THE CURTAIN THEATRE. STAGE. DAY.

The audience waits expectantly. WABASH gathers himself.

WABASH AS THE CHORUS

T-t-t-t-two . . .

INT. THE CURTAIN THEATRE. BACKSTAGE. DAY.

WILL shuts his eyes and prays.

INT. THE CURTAIN THEATRE. STAGE/AUDITORIUM. DAY.

WABASH launches himself into a perfect audacious delivery like a star.

WABASH AS THE CHORUS

" . . . Households both alike in dignity
(in fair Verona where we lay our scene)
From ancient grudge break to new mutiny,
Where civil blood makes civil hands unclean.
From forth the fatal loins of these two foes

A pair of star-cross'd lovers take their life,
Whose misadventured piteous overthrows
Doth with their death bury their parents' strife . . . "

EXT. STREET. DAY.

VIOLA and the NURSE, hurrying toward the Curtain.

INT. THE CURTAIN THEATRE. BACKSTAGE. DAY.

HEMMINGS BROTHERS are ready to go on as "SAMPSON" and "GREGORY," Act I Scene I. They shake hands. Beyond the curtain, the audience applauds the Prologue as WABASH comes through the curtain backstage.

WILL
(to WABASH)
Wonderful!

WABASH
W-w-w-was it g-g-g-good?

The HEMMINGS BROTHERS enter the arena and the play begins.

POV: from THE WINGS:

JOHN HEMMINGS AS SAMPSON
"Gregory, on my word we'll not carry coals."

JAMES HEMMINGS AS GREGORY
"No, for then we should be colliers."

WILL looks as if he would rather be dead. SAM GOSSE approaches WILL, nervously.

SAM
(nervously—in a deep bass guttural hoarse voice)
Master Shakespeare . . .

WILL

(absently)

Luck be with you, Sam.

(as the awful truth gets through to him)

Sam . . . ?

SAM

(in the same voice)

It is not my fault, Master Shakespeare. I could do it yesterday.

WILL

Sam! Do me a speech, do me a line.

SAM

(the effect is horrible)

"Parting is such sweet sorrow . . . "

HENSLOWE has been overhearing.

HENSLOWE

Another little problem.

WILL

What do we do now?

HENSLOWE

The show must . . . you know . . .

WILL

Go on.

HENSLOWE

Juliet does not come on for twenty pages. It will be all right.

WILL

How will it?

HENSLOWE

I don't know. It's a mystery.

And he makes his way towards the front of the house.

EXT. STREET. DAY.

A furious WESSEX is hurrying along the road to the theatre.

INT. THE CURTAIN THEATRE. AUDITORIUM/STAGE. DAY.

VIOLA and the NURSE are arriving, and looking for a seat in the gallery. BURBAGE and his MEN are standing at the back, behind the people seated in the gallery. The first scene of the play is continuing . . .

ARMITAGE AS ABRAM

"Do you bite your thumb at us, sir?"

JOHN HEMMINGS AS SAMPSON

"I do bite my thumb, sir."

BURBAGE finds HENSLOWE plucking agitatedly at his sleeve.

HENSLOWE

Can we talk?

They are standing behind the back row of the gallery seats. The spectator in front of them is the NURSE. She turns round and shushes HENSLOWE up.

HENSLOWE (Cont'd)
(whispering to BURBAGE)

We have no Juliet!

BURBAGE
(forgetting to whisper)

No Juliet?!

VIOLA
(turning)

No Juliet?!

HENSLOWE

It will be all right, madam.

VIOLA

What happened to Sam?

HENSLOWE

Who are you?

VIOLA

Thomas Kent!

Their whispers are causing black looks and hushing noises from the neighbours. HENSLOWE pulls VIOLA from her seat, luckily an aisle seat.

HENSLOWE

Do you know it?

VIOLA
(showing the manuscript)

Every word.

HENSLOWE and BURBAGE look at each other. CUT TO:

INT. THE CURTAIN THEATRE. STAGE. DAY.

PHILIPS AS LADY CAPULET

"Nurse, where is my daughter? Call her forth to me."

RALPH AS NURSE

"Now by my maidenhead at twelve year old,
I bade her come. What, lamb. What ladybird."

INT. THE CURTAIN THEATRE. THE WINGS/STAGE. DAY.

SAM who gathers himself, to make his entrance, quietly and horribly practising "How now, who calls?"

RALPH AS NURSE
(on stage)
"God forbid. Where's this girl? . . .

The author and star, WILL SHAKESPEARE, has his back to the stage, his hands over his ears. He is cowering in dread anticipation.

RALPH AS NURSE (Cont'd)
. . . "What, Juliet!"

As SAM is about to enter HENSLOWE'S hand yanks him by the collar, and VIOLA overtakes him and steps on stage. Enter "JULIET." VIOLA is not wearing the "JULIET" costume— she is wearing her own beautiful dress, which up till now has been hidden from us by her cloak.

VIOLA AS JULIET
"How now, who calls?"

RALPH AS NURSE
"Your mother."

VIOLA AS JULIET
"Madam. I am here, what is your will?"

INT. THE CURTAIN THEATRE. AUDITORIUM. DAY.

There is a collective gasp. Nobody has ever seen a BOY PLAYER like this.

INT. THE CURTAIN THEATRE. THE WINGS. DAY.

WILL takes his hands from his ears, and turns round in amazement at the sound of

VIOLA'S voice.

INT. THE CURTAIN THEATRE. AUDITORIUM/STAGE. DAY.

WESSEX has just arrived in the auditorium and jumps as if he has been shot. He seems about to intervene, but looking around at the rapt faces he realises he cannot.

INT. THE CURTAIN THEATRE. THE WINGS. DAY.

HENSLOWE and BURBAGE look at each other.

BURBAGE

We will all be put in the clink.

HENSLOWE

(shrugs)

See you in jail.

INT. THE CURTAIN THEATRE. BACKSTAGE. DAY.

FENNYMAN, oblivious to the drama, is practising his lines in a fever of nervousness.

FENNYMAN

"Such mortal drugs I have but Mantua's law

Is death to any he that utters them."
Then him. Then me.

INT. THE CURTAIN THEATRE. STAGE. DAY.

Swordplay. An amazing performance that holds the audience spellbound. "TYBALT" kills "MERCUTIO."

ALLEYN AS MERCUTIO
(to ROMEO)

"I am hurt.

WILL AS ROMEO

Courage man. The hurt cannot be much.

ALLEYN AS MERCUTIO

Ask for me tomorrow and you shall find me a grave man."

A roll of thunder. Over the heads of the audience, far above the thatched roof of the theatre, clouds are gathering in the sky. On stage "MERCUTIO" is in "ROMEO'S" arms, but the tone of the playing is unlike anything we have seen before: without bombast, intense and real. And the audience is quiet and attentive.

ALLEYN AS MERCUTIO (Cont'd)

" . . .—Why the devil came you between us? I was hurt under your arm."

EXT. THE CURTAIN THEATRE. DAY.

In the semirural view towards the City of London, there can be discerned a gaggle of approaching MEN and there is something orderly about them. As they come closer, we see that they are a company of PIKE MEN, marching toward the theatre, led by the Master of the Revels, TILNEY. Thunder rolls.

INT. THE CURTAIN THEATRE. STAGE. DAY.

Figures are running across the stage, in the panic that follows "TYBALT'S" death.

ACTOR AS BENVOLIO

"Romeo, away, be gone!
The citizens are up and Tybalt slain.
Stand not amazed. The prince will doom thee death
If thou art taken.
Hence, be gone away!"

WILL AS ROMEO

"I am fortune's fool!"

ACTOR AS BENVOLIO

"Why dost thou stay!"

INT. THE CURTAIN THEATRE. BACKSTAGE. DAY.

WILL has just 'killed' "TYBALT." He is still breathless from fighting. He stands face to face with VIOLA.

WILL

I am fortune's fool.

They stare at each other, transfixed

WILL (Cont'd)

You are married?

PAUSE. She cannot answer.

WILL (Cont'd)

If you be married, my grave is like to be my wedding bed.

The implication of her silence fills the air. WILL does not move.

INT. THE CURTAIN THEATRE. STAGE. DAY.

We cannot tell whether this is the play or their life. The audience, and the rest of the world, might as well not exist. WILL turns from her and begins to descend from the 'balcony.'

VIOLA AS JULIET

"Art thou gone so? . . .

WILL stops.

VIOLA AS JULIET (Cont'd)

. . . Love, lord, ay husband, friend,
I must hear from thee every day in the hour,
For in a minute there are many days.
O, by this count I shall be much in years
Ere I again behold my Romeo . . . "

WILL as "ROMEO" seems unable to speak. Then he says:

WILL AS ROMEO

" . . . Farewell . . . "

All other sounds drain away, and time seems to stop.

VIOLA AS JULIET

"O think'st thou we shall ever meet again . . . ?
Methinks I see thee, now thou art so low,
As one dead in the bottom of a tomb.
Either my eyesight fails, or thou lookest pale."

WILL AS ROMEO

"Trust me, love, in my eyes so do you.
Dry sorrow drinks our blood. Adieu. Adieu"

INT. THE CURTAIN THEATRE. STAGE. DAY.

Now the FRIAR is giving "JULIET" his potion.

EDWARD AS FRIAR

"No warmth, no breath shall testify thou livest . . .
And in this borrow'd likeness of shrunk death
Thou shall continue two and forty hours
And then awake as from a pleasant sleep . . . "

INT. THE CURTAIN THEATRE. STAGE. DAY.

It's FENNYMAN'S moment. The "APOTHECARY" and "ROMEO."

WILL AS ROMEO

"Come hither, man. I see that thou art poor.
Hold, there is forty ducats. Let me have
A dram of poison—"

FENNYMAN AS APOTHECARY

"Such mortal drugs I have but Mantua's law
is death to any he that utters them!"

FENNYMAN has cut in several lines early, but his conviction is astonishing.

FENNYMAN AS APOTHECARY

"My poverty but not my will consents."

WILL AS ROMEO

"I pay thy poverty and not thy will."

EXT. STREET. NEAR THE CURTAIN THEATRE. DAY.

TILNEY, on the march. His hand grips a copy of the Curtain flyer.

INT. THE CURTAIN THEATRE. STAGE. DAY.

"JULIET" lies "dead." She lies on top of her tomb, "lying in state," her best dress, her hair done, her hands in prayer at her breast, her eyes closed. "ROMEO" has found her like this.

WILL AS ROMEO

"Eyes, look your last!
Arms, take your last embrace! and lips, Oh you
The doors of breath, seal with a righteous kiss
A dateless bargain to engrossing death!
Come, bitter conduct; come, unsavory guide!
Thou desparate pilot, now at once run on
The dashing rocks thy seasick weary bark!"

As WILL embraces her, VIOLA'S eyes flicker open (shielded by WILL from the audience) and the lovers look at each other for a moment as WILL and VIOLA rather than as "ROMEO" and "JULIET." Their eyes are wet with tears.

INT. THE CURTAIN THEATRE. AUDITORIUM. DAY.

BURBAGE and ROSALINE are watching.

INT. THE CURTAIN THEATRE. AUDITORIUM. DAY.

KEMPE is watching.

INT. THE CURTAIN THEATRE. AUDITORIUM. DAY.

We see that in the audience are several of the WHORES we recognise from the brothel. They are weeping openly.

INT. THE CURTAIN THEATRE. STAGE. DAY.

WILL is raising the fatal drug in a last toast.

WILL AS ROMEO

"Here's to my love

(he drinks)

O true Apothecary."

INT. THE CURTAIN THEATRE. THE WINGS. DAY.

FENNYMAN, moved but proud in the wings.

FENNYMAN

(whispers to himself)

I was good. I was great.

INT. THE CURTAIN THEATRE. STAGE. DAY.

WILL AS ROMEO

"Thy drugs are quick. Thus with a kiss I die."

(and he dies)

INT. THE CURTAIN THEATRE. AUDITORIUM. DAY.

The NURSE is weeping too.

INT. THE CURTAIN THEATRE. STAGE. DAY.

"JULIET" wakes up with a start.

VIOLA AS JULIET

" . . . Where is my lord?
I do remember well where I should be,
And there I am. Where is my Romeo?"

INT. THE CURTAIN THEATRE. AUDITORIUM. DAY.

NURSE

(involuntarily)

Dead!

INT. THE CURTAIN THEATRE. STAGE. DAY.

VIOLA AS JULIET

"What's here? A cup clos'd in my true love's hand?
Poison, I see, hath been his timeless end."

INT. THE CURTAIN THEATRE. STAGE. DAY.

"JULIET" takes "ROMEO'S" dagger.

VIOLA AS JULIET

" . . . O happy dagger
This is thy sheath. There rust, and let me die."

She stabs herself and dies. The "inner curtain" closes over the tomb.

INT. THE CURTAIN THEATRE. STAGE/AUDITORIUM DAY.

HIGH ANGLE on audience and stage. "THE PRINCE" played by WABASH is having the last word.

THE PRINCE

"For never was a story of more woe
Than this of Juliet and her Romeo."

The end. There is complete silence. The ACTORS are worried. But then the audience goes mad with applause.

INT. THE CURTAIN THEATRE. THE INNER CURTAIN/STAGE. DAY.

The inner curtain opens, but WILL and VIOLA, are in a play of their own . . . embracing and kissing passionately, making their own farewell.

HENSLOWE is too stunned and moved to react at first. Then he looks at the audience and the penny drops. It's a hit.

INT. THE CURTAIN THEATRE. AUDITORIUM/STAGE. DAY.

The audience roars. WILL, VIOLA, and THE COMPANY come forward to meet the applause. TILNEY and his MEN burst in. TILNEY jumps up onto the stage, where the ADMIRAL'S MEN are taking their bows. TILNEY'S "COPS" ring the stage, facing inwards.

TILNEY
(shouts triumphantly)
I arrest you in the name of Queen Elizabeth!

The AUDIENCE goes quiet. BURBAGE jumps out of the audience onto the stage.

BURBAGE
Arrest who, Mr. Tilney?

TILNEY
Everybody! The Admiral's Men, The Chamberlain's Men and every one of you ne'er-do-wells who stands in contempt of the authority invested in me by her Majesty.

BURBAGE
Contempt? You closed the Rose—I have not opened it.

TILNEY is at a loss but only for a moment.

TILNEY
(he points a "j'accuse" finger at VIOLA)
That woman is a woman!

The entire audience and the actors, recoil and gasp. The NURSE crosses herself.

ALLEYN

What?! A woman?! You mean that goat?!

He points at VIOLA, brazening it out without much chance.

TILNEY

I'll see you all in the clink! In the name of her Majesty Queen Elizabeth—

And an authoritative voice from the audience interrupts him.

VOICE

Mr. Tilney . . . !

It is QUEEN ELIZABETH herself, descending now, her hood and cloak thrown back. She is an awesome sight. A shaft of sunlight hits her.

QUEEN

Have a care with my name, you will wear it out.

There is a general parting of the waves, soldiers and actors, a general backing off and bowing as QUEEN ELIZABETH takes the limelight.

QUEEN (Cont'd)

The Queen of England does not attend exhibitions of public lewdness so something is out of joint. Come here, Master Kent. Let me look at you.

VIOLA comes forward, and is about to curtsey when she catches the QUEEN'S eye, an arresting eye, which arrests the curtsey and turns it into a sweeping bow.

QUEEN (Cont'd)

Yes, the illusion is remarkable and your error, Mr. Tilney, is easily forgiven, but I know something of a woman in a man's profession, yes, by God, I do know about that. That is enough from you, Master Kent. If only Lord Wessex were here!

VOICE

He is, Ma'am.

The voice belongs to JOHN WEBSTER. He points firmly at a figure in the audience, WESSEX, trying to look inconspicuous.

WESSEX

(weakly)

Your Majesty . . .

QUEEN

There was a wager, I remember . . . as to whether a play can show the very truth and nature of love. I think you lost it today.

(turning to WEBSTER)

You are an eager boy. Did you like the play?

WEBSTER

I liked it when she stabbed herself, your Majesty.

The QUEEN fixes WILL with a beady eye.

QUEEN

Master Shakespeare. Next time you come to Greenwich, come as yourself and we will speak some more.

WILL bows deeply. The QUEEN turns to leave. The waves part for her.

INT. THE CURTAIN THEATRE. MAIN ENTRANCE. DAY.

The QUEEN is bowed out through the doors.

EXT. THE CURTAIN THEATRE. DAY.

A gaggle of the QUEEN'S favoured courtiers wait by her carriage. WESSEX is hurrying down the exterior staircase as the QUEEN emerges from the theatre. During the following a general egress from the auditorium is taking place, including some of the actors crowding to see her off.

WESSEX bows out of breath.

WESSEX

Your Majesty!

QUEEN

Why, Lord Wessex! Lost your wife so soon?

WESSEX

Indeed I am a bride short. How is this to end?

VIOLA has come out of the theatre, amongst some of the other players. The QUEEN catches her eye.

QUEEN

As stories must when love's denied— with tears and a journey. Those whom God has joined in marriage, not even I can put asunder.

QUEEN (Cont'd)

(she turns to VIOLA)

Lord Wessex, as I foretold, has lost his wife in the playhouse—go make your farewell and send her out. It's time to settle accounts.

(to WESSEX)

How much was the wager?

WESSEX

Fifty shillings.

(the QUEEN gives him a look)

Pounds.

QUEEN

Give it to Master Kent. He will see it rightfully home.

WESSEX gives his purse to VIOLA

QUEEN (Cont'd)

(to VIOLA)

And tell Shakespeare something more cheerful next time, for Twelfth Night.

The QUEEN proceeds towards her carriage. There is an enormous puddle between her and her carriage. The QUEEN hesitates for a fraction and then marches through the puddle as cloaks descend upon it.

QUEEN (Cont'd)

Too late, too late.

She splashes her way into her carriage, which departs.

INT. THE CURTAIN THEATRE. STAGE. DAY.

WILL

(heartbroken; testing her name)

My Lady Wessex?

VIOLA nods, heartbroken too. For a long moment they cannot say anything to each other. Then she holds up Wessex's purse.

VIOLA

A hired player no longer. Fifty pounds, Will, for the poet of true love.

WILL

I am done with theatre. The playhouse is for dreamers. Look where the dream has brought us.

VIOLA

It was we ourselves did that. And for my life to come I would not have it otherwise.

WILL

I have hurt you and I am sorry for it.

VIOLA

If my hurt is to be that you will write no more, then I shall be the sorrier.

WILL looks at her

VIOLA (Cont'd)

The Queen commands a comedy, Will, for Twelfth Night.

WILL

(harshly)

A comedy! What will my hero be but the saddest wretch in the kingdom, sick with love?

VIOLA

An excellent beginning . . .

(a beat)

Let him be . . . a duke. And your heroine?

WILL

(bitterly)

Sold in marriage and half way to America

VIOLA

(adjusting)

At sea, then—a voyage to a new world? . . . she lands upon a vast and empty shore. She is brought to the duke . . . Orsino

WILL

(despite himself)

. . . Orsino . . . good name . . .

VIOLA

But fearful of her virtue, she comes to him dressed as a boy . . .

WILL

(Catching it)

. . . and thus unable to declare her love . . .

Pause. They look at each other. Suddenly the conversation seems to be about them.

VIOLA

But all ends well.

WILL

How does it?

VIOLA

I don't know. It's a mystery.

WILL half smiles. Then he's serious. They look deeply at each other . . . and rush into each other's arms.

WILL (Cont'd)

You will never age for me, nor fade, nor die.

VIOLA

Nor you for me.

WILL

Good bye, my love, a thousand times good bye.

VIOLA

Write me well.

She kisses him with finality. Then turns and runs from him. WILL watches as she goes.

INT. WILL'S ROOM. DAY.

A blank page. A hand is writing: TWELFTH NIGHT. We see WILL sitting at his table.

WILL (VO)

My story starts at sea . . . a perilous voyage to an unknown land . . . a shipwreck . . .

EXT. UNDERWATER. DAY.

Two figures plunge into the water . . .

WILL (VO)

. . . the wild waters roar and heave . . . the brave vessel is dashed all to pieces, and all the helpless souls within her drowned . . .

INT. WILL'S ROOM. DAY.

WILL at his table writing . . .

WILL (VO)

. . . all save one . . . a lady . . .

EXT. UNDERWATER. DAY.

VIOLA in the water . . .

WILL (VO)

. . . whose soul is greater than the ocean . . . and her spirit stronger than the sea's embrace . . . not for her a watery end, but a new life beginning on a stranger shore . . .

EXT. BEACH. DAY.

VIOLA is walking up a vast and empty beach . . . .

WILL (VO CONTINUED)

It will be a love story . . . for she will be my heroine for all time . . .

INT. WILL'S ROOM. DAY.

WILL looks up from the table

WILL (VO CONTINUED)

. . . and her name will be . . . Viola.

He looks down at the paper, and writes: "Viola"

Then: "What country friends is this?"

EXT. BEACH. DAY

DISSOLVE slowly to VIOLA, walking away up the beach towards her brave new world.

THE END

Miramax Films Universal Pictures
Bedford Falls Company
present

SHAKESPEARE IN LOVE

Directed by
John Madden

Written by
Marc Norman and Tom Stoppard

Produced by
David Parfitt
Donna Gigliotti
Harvey Weinstein
Edward Zwick
Marc Norman

Executive Producers
Bob Weinstein
Julie Goldstein

Line Producer
Mark Cooper

Director of Photography
Richard Greatrex, B.S.C.

Production Designer
Martin Childs

Editor
David Gamble

Costume Designer
Sandy Powell

Music by
Stephen Warbeck

Make Up and Hair Design
Lisa Westcott

Casting
Michelle Guish

A film by John Madden

CAST IN ORDER OF APPEARANCE

Philip Henslowe	Geoffrey Rush
Hugh Fennyman	Tom Wilkinson
Lambert	Steven O'Donnell
Frees	Tim McMullen
Will Shakespeare	Joseph Fiennes
Makepeace, the Preacher	Steven Beard
Dr Moth	Antony Sher
Will Kempe	Patrick Barlow
Richard Burbage	Martin Clunes
Rosaline	Sandra Reinton
Tilney, Master of the Revels	Simon Callow
Queen Elizabeth	Judi Dench
Ladies in Waiting	Bridget McConnel
	Georgie Glen
Henry Condell	Nicholas Boulton
Viola De Lesseps	Gwyneth Paltrow
Nurse	Imelda Staunton
Lord Wessex	Colin Firth
Crier	Desmond McNamara
Nol	Barnaby Kay
Ralph Bashford	Jim Carter
Peter, the Stage Manager	Paul Bigley
Actor in Tavern	Jason Round
Barman	Rupert Farley
First Auditionee	Adam Barker
John Webster	Joe Roberts
Second Auditionee	Harry Gostelow
Third Auditionee	Alan Cody
Wabash	Mark Williams
John Hemmings	David Curtiz
James Hemmings	Gregor Truter
First Boatman	Simon Day
Lady De Lesseps	Jill Baker
Scullery Maid	Amber Glossop
Master Plum	Robin Davies
Servant	Hywel Simons

Sir Robert De Lesseps	Nicholas Le Prevost
Ned Alleyn	Ben Affleck
Edward Pope	Timothy Kightley
Augustine Philips	Mark Saban
George Bryan	Bob Barrett
James Armitage	Roger Morlidge
Sam Gosse	Daniel Brocklebank
Second Boatman	Roger Frost
Chambermaid	Rebecca Charles
Lord in Waiting	Richard Gold
First Whore	Rachel Clarke
Second Whore	Lucy Speed
Third Whore	Patricia Potter
Makepeace's Neighbour	John Ramm
Paris/Lady Montague	Martin Neeley

The Choir of St George's School, Windsor

First Assistant Director	Deborah Saban
Financial Controller	Liz Barron
Script Supervisor	Kim Armitage
Production Sound Mixer	Peter Glossop
Set Decorator	Jill Quertier
Supervising Art Director	Mark Raggett
Assistant Costume Designer	Deborah Scott
Location Manager	Rachel Neale
Production Co-ordinator	Fiona Weir
Post Production Co-ordinator	Cleone Clarke
Dialogue Coach	Barbara Berkery
Fight Arranger	William Hobbs
Choreographer	Quinny Sacks
Script Editor	Irena Brignull
US Casting	Billy Hopkins
	Suzanne Smith
	Kerry Barden
Second Assistant Director	Olivia Lloyd
Second Second Assistant Director	Tom Gabbutt

Third Assistant Director	Toby Hefferman
Art Director	Steve Lawrence
Property Buyer	Gill Ducker
Storyboard Artist	Jane Clark
Standby Art Director	Frances Bennett
Draughtsmen	Matt Gray
	Keith Pain
Art Department Assistant	Christine Parkin
Scenic Artist	Steve Sallybanks
Camera Operator	Philip Sindall
Focus Puller	Brad Larner
Clapper Loader	Ed Rutherford
Grip	Pat Garrett
Camera Trainee	Kirsty Argyle
FT2 Grip Assistant	John McSweeney
First Assistant Editor	Christine Campbell
Second Assistant Editor	Julian Pryce
Trainee Editor	Jonathan Haren
Additional First Assistant Editors	Kate Higham
	Robert Laycock
Supervising Sound Editor	John Downer
Dialogue Editor	Sarah Morton
ADR Editor	Brigitte Arnold
Foley Editor	Howard Eaves
Foley Mixed by	Ken Somerville
Foley Artistes	Pauline Griffiths
	Paula Boram
	Jenny Lee Wright
Additional Sound Editor	Colin Chapman
Preview Re-Recording Mixer	Ian Tapp
Re-Recording Mixers	Robin O'Donoghue
	Dominic Lester
Boom Operator	Shaun Mills

Sound Maintenance	Stephen Gilmour
Music Supervision	Maggie Rodford and
	Becky Bentham
	Air Edel Associates Limited
Music Editor	Roy Prendergast
Conductor	Nick Ingman
Orchestrations	Stephen Warbeck
	Nick Ingman
Additional Orchestrations	James Shearman
Orchestra Leader	Gavyn Wright
Music Recorded and Mixed by	Chris Dibble
Assisted by	Erik Jordan
Soprano Soloist	Catherine Bott
Music Recorded and Mixed at	CTS Studios, London
Musicians' Contractor	Isobel Wright
Copyist	Tony Stanton
Composer's Assistant	Andrew Green
Property Master	Danny Hunter
Property Storeman	Paul Turner
Chargehand Dressing Props	Kevin Wheeler
Dressing Props	Ian Fryer
	Nathan Turner
Chargehand Standby Propsman	Colin Mutch
Standby Propsman	Les Andrews
Props Trainee	Chris Arnold
Gaffer	Steve Costello
Best Boy	Alfie Emmins
Electricians	Ross Chapman
	Warren Evans
	Dave Moore
	Paul Wood
Sparks Rigger	Tom Lowen
	Jason Curtis
Costume Supervisor	Clare Spragge

Wardrobe Assistants	Sunita Singh
	Dan Grace
	Andrew Hunt
	Sophie Norinder
	Joe Kowalewski
	Jenny Hawkins
Costume Buyers	Kay Manasseh
	Emma Fryer
Chief Costume Cutters and Makers	Annie Hadley
	Jane Law
	Ruth Caswell
	Claire Christie
	Alison O'Brien
	Debbie Marchant
Milliner	Sean Barrett
Costume Makers	Clare Banet
	Melanie Carter
	Gill Crawford
	Heather Dickins
	Linda Lashley
	Ruth McCornish
	Tanya Mould
	Susan Stevens
	Joanna Weaving
	Sue Bradbear
	Wendy Cole
	Sue Crawshaw
	Jane Grimshaw
	Wayne Martin
	Sue Meyer
	Marcia Smith
	Roslyn Tiddy
	Dominic Young
Shoes Supplied By	Pompei
	Gamba
Jewellery Supplied by	Gioielli L.A.B.A. Roma
Costumes Supplied by	Angels and Bermans

	Cornejo
	Costumi D'Arte-Roma
Makeup Designer for Gwyneth Paltrow	Tina Earnshaw
Hair Designer for Gwyneth Paltrow	Kay Georgiou
Senior Hair & Makeup Artist	Veronica Brebner
Hair & Makeup Artists	Julie Dartnell
	Karen Ferguson
	Philippa Hall
	Deborah Jarvis
	Lesley Smith
Wigs Supplied by	Ray Marston Wig Studio
	BBC Wig Store
Assistant Accountant/Post Production Accountant	Margaret Teatum
Art Department Accountant	Helen Manley
Cashier	Tabitha Burrill
Unit Manager	Samantha Thomas
Stills Photographer	Laurie Sparham
Unit Publicist	Zoë Mylchreest
EPK	Feasible Films
Assistant to David Parfitt	Cleone Clarke
Assistant to Donna Gigliotti	Zelda Perkins
Assistant to John Madden	Nicki Sung
Assistant to Gwyneth Paltrow	Sophie Shand
Assistant to Geoffrey Rush	Jami Wrenn
Assitants to Harvey Weinstein	Rick Schwartz
	Barbara Schneeweiss
	Rebecca Heller
	Mark Friedman
Assistants to Bob Weinstein	Louis Spiegler
	Michael Neithardt
Assistant to Julie Goldstein	Meighan Dobson

Miramax/UK Co-ordinators	Zelda Perkins
	Iain York
Production Assistant	Catherine Jardine
Production Runner	Jon McCrory
Floor Runners	Mari Roberts
	Nicholas Du Boulay
	Carlos Fidel
Construction Manager	Andy Evans
Assistant Construction Manager	Ian Green
Construction Buyer	Robert Allen
Supervising Carpenters	Dave Edwards
	Gary Pledger
Supervising Painters	John Campbell
	Paul Wiltshire
Supervising Rigger	Peter Graffham
Supervising Stagehand	Colin Smith
Chargehand Stagehand	Brian Webb
Sculptor	Fred Evans
Assistant Sculptor	Tracy Ann Baines
Carpenters	John Addison
	Steve Alder
	Joe Alley
	Michael Biesty
	Darryl Carter
	Joe Cassar
	Chris Corke
	Martin Day
	John Franklin
	Lee Gooch
	Michael Gooch
	Frederick Gunning
	Ralph Harrison
	Darren Hayward
	Frank Henry
	Andrew Hobbs
	Nick Lloyd

	Hugh McKenzie
	Anthony Mansey
	Danny Margetts
	Christopher Mansey
	Andrew Mash
	Peter Murray
	Steve Murray
	Reg Patterson
	James Reid
	Lee Reilly
	Bernard Ryan
	Barry Smalls
	Dean Smith
	Tony Snook
	Paul Woods
	Stuart Williams
	Robert Wright
Painters	Stuart Blinco
	Adam Campbell
	Glyn Evans
	Anthony Goddard
	Giovanni Giacotto
	Lee Goddard
	Graham Pearce
	Ted Restall
	John Shergold
	Clive Whitbread
	Steven Sibley
Painter's Labourer	Harry Alley
	Robert Stagg
Riggers	Trevor Carey
	Raymond Flindall
	Mark Goldeman
	Robert Diebelius
	Mark Fox-Potten
	Martin Goddard
	Ronald Miles
	Jose Romero

	Joe Russo
	Reg Smith
Stagehands	Michael Bailey
	Raymond Branch
	Steven Bovingdon
	Trevor Carey
	Larry Rashbrook
	Danny Smith
	Roy Smith
	Michael Webb
Stand by Carpenters	John Casey
Stand by Painter	Brian Groves
Stand by Riggers	Paul Mills
Stand by Stagehand	Clifford Rashbrook
Special Effects	United Special Effects
Special Effects Supervisor	Stuart Brisdon
Titles Design	Shaun Webb Design
Extras Casting	Julian Carter & Ilenka Jelowicki at 20/20
Stand-ins	Colette Appleby
	Steve Morphew
	David Oliver
Horse Co-ordinator	Debbie Kaye
Animals Supplied By	Animals OK
Computers Supplied by	AJM Systems
Boats Supplied by	Turk Film Services Ltd
Marquees Supplied by	Witney Marquees
	Marquees Over London
Health and Safety Advisor	Paul Jackson
Rehearsal Stage Manager	Christine Hathway
Text Consultant	Russell Jackson
Performance Consultant	Philip Wilson

Verse Consultant	Andrew Wade
Casting Assistant	Gaby Kester

SECOND UNIT

Second Unit Director	Arthur Wooster BSC
Camera Operator	Tim Wooster
Steadicam Operator	Vince McGahon
Underwater Unit Co-ordinator & Cameraman	Mike Valentine
Focus Puller	John Gamble
Clapper Loader	Ian Coffey
Sound Recordist	Clive Copland
Boom Operator	Keith Batten
Script Supervisor	Caroline Sax
Stuntmen	Paul Jennings
	David Cronelly
	Phil Lonergan
	Mark Mottram
	Gabe Cronelly
	Mark Southworth
	Seon Rogers
	Paul Herbert

VISUAL EFFECTS UNIT

Visual Effects Supervisor	Antony Hunt
Digital Supervisor	Angus Cameron
Domino Artist	Dan Pettipher
Digital Matte Artist	Max Dennison
2D Digital Artist	Robin Huffer
Digital & Optical Co-ordinator	Andrew Jeffrey
Digital Film Scanning	John Grant
Camera Operator	Rick Mietkowski
Focus Puller	Andrew Stevens
Loader	Matthew d'Angibau
Production Assistant	Tori Martin

Transport Captain	Barry Leonti
Unit Drivers	Brian Agar
	Mike Crawley

	Len Furssedonn
	Paul Grahame
	Georg Grohmann
	Jim Magill
	Simon Saunders
	John Smith
	Harry Smith
Transport Manager	Tony Bird
	at Aeroshoot Film Services
Camera Driver	Rob Fowle
Wardrobe Vehicle Driver	Ian Maskell
Makeup Vehicle Driver	Jeff Derby
Props Stand By Vehicle Driver	Kieran Smith
Dressing Props Vehicle Driver	Phil Foley
Dining Bus Driver	Jimmy Coutts
Honeywagon Driver	Bert Berry
Construction Stand By Vehicle Driver	John Cornelius
	at Cavalier Transport
Construction Vehicle Driver	Mark Russell
Minibus Driver	David Gwyther
Caterers	Set Meals
Unit Nurses	Katherine Teakle
Camera Equipment Supplied by	Arri Film Media Service Ltd
	Dolby Digital
Film Stock Supplied By	KODAK
Lighting Equipment Supplied by	Lee Lighting
Editing Equipment Supplied by	Hyperactive
	London Editing Machines Ltd
Film Opticals	Cine Image
Colour Processing	Deluxe Laboratories Ltd
Grader	Michael Stainer
Negative Cutter	Sylvia Wheeler Film Services
Foley Mixed at	Anvil Post Production

Re-Recording Mixed at Shepperton Sound
Dolby Sound Consultant James Seddon

Post Production Scripts Sapex Scripts
Transfers at Telefilm
The Machine Room
Midnight Transfer

Production Insurance by AON/Albert G Reuben
Legal Advisors Olswang
Travel Arranged by Check In for Business

Filmed at
SHEPPERTON STUDIOS LONDON ENGLAND
and on location in England at
Broughton Castle, Banbury (Great Hall, Middle Temple
Eton College (The Church of St Bartholomew The Great (Marble Hill House
Holkham Beach and Estate, Norfolk

Thanks To
Casey Silver Chris McGurk Meryl Poster Jon Gumpert
John Logigian Marshall Herskovitz Paul Webster
Henry Braham Dr Stephen Greenblatt Lord & Lady Saye and Sele
Paul Olliver Denis Carrigan Neil Mockler Clive Noakes

Special Thanks To
Mick Audsley Robin Sales

In memory of
Jane Annakin
Mathilde Sandberg

MPAA No 36421
Miramax Films / Universal Pictures